CRATE CRAFT

By Lura LaBarge
Illustrations and Diagrams by Lura LaBarge
Projects Built by George W. Beierle

CRATE CRAFT

EASY-TO-MAKE FURNITURE AND ACCESSORIES YOU CAN BUILD QUICKLY AND INEXPENSIVELY

Butterick Publishing

Color Photography by Robin Forbes
Book Design by Bob Antler
Cover Design by Winifred Young

Library of Congress Catalog Card Number: 76-9185
International Standard Book Number: 0-88421-053-7

Copyright © 1976 by Butterick Publishing
161 Sixth Avenue   New York, New York 10013

A Division of American Can Company

Printed in U.S.A

to Leo M. and Leo R.

ACKNOWLEDGMENTS

For their assistance in providing information and materials used in building the pieces shown on these pages, I want to thank Mr. Edward Benfield of the Stanley Works; Mr. Dave Sundstedt of the Amerock Corporation (cabinet hardware); Mr. Jeff Falini of Angelo Brothers Company (Lamparts® lighting supplies); Mr. John Gill of Rohm and Haas (Plexiglas®); and especially Mr. and Mrs. Richard K. Myers of The Silo for saving the crates from countless pianos and organs for me.

I owe many thanks to Mr. Robert Kaplan, Builder-Developer of Janro Realty, for permission to use one of his model homes for setting up the furniture for photography and to Mr. Michael Steinhardt, Construction Supervisor, for making it work. Decorative accessories were supplied by Mr. and Mrs. Ralph deVries (plants); Ms. Britt Puleo (rugs); Mr. and Mrs. Paul Desmet (owners "Pegasus" macrame hanging); Mr. John Ashback of TACC Industries (mini-crates); Ms. Betty Platt of Lamp Lighters of LaFayette (advice and selection of lampshades); and thanks go especially to Evelyn Brannon for making the cushions for chair, loveseat and footstool.

I want to thank Mr. George W. Beierle for his pleasant cooperation and boundless energy in translating my preliminary drawings into functioning furniture pieces. His comments were invaluable in simplifying still further certain of the original designs.

CONTENTS

CRATE CRAFT

INTRODUCTION

No magic exists to turn crates into furniture. It takes plotting, planning and work. This book is not about how to stack boxes and call them bookshelves. It does suggest ways to find, process and use crating and other scrap lumber to build home furnishings of which you can be proud.

Creating something from nothing is a great idea. You can acquire the know-how it takes to convert other people's rubbish into useful pieces for your home. You will learn by looking at and working with growing confidence in your carpentry skills with whatever wood you can find. We include not only a list of tools you'll need but tips on how to use them most effectively. Working with wood requires the sort of judgment that really comes through experience. We'll try to show you some shortcuts. There are hardware items that can make construction easier and we'll tell you about some of them, too. The plans presented here are adaptable to different thicknesses and widths of wood. We show you how to think projects through so they will work for you.

You could go out and buy ¾" top-quality plywood and build your furniture exactly to a pattern that tells you precisely where to cut, what kind and how many nails to use with what kind of glue and how many coats of which finish works best. These "pattern books" usually assume you have a basement full of power tools and know how to use each and every one of them.

You can't do that type of precision work with crating lumber. It is much more creative. You have to do some of the thinking. Once you have an understanding of the possibilities and the range of usefulness, you can do it. You'll start out with an idea of the piece you want to build and then look around to see what kind of crates are available. Using what you can learn here, the end result will come somewhere near fulfilling your needs and desires. We don't claim it is simple. We do claim it can be fun. And whatever the result, there is one thing you will have the satisfaction of knowing — nowhere is there another piece exactly like the one you made yourself.

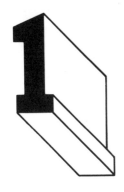

ROUNDING UP
THE PIECES

WHERE TO LOOK

Scrounging can be an educational experience. You'll soon see how wasteful our civilization is, and you'll meet a lot of interesting people you'd never have spoken to otherwise. The chances of finding a crate of a size you can use as is are mighty slim. Chances of finding lumber you can salvage to advantage are really great. Even though the modern packaging industry has changed the face of the loading dock, there is still a lot of lumber in the throw-out pile waiting to be recycled.

Almost twice as much lumber went into packaging as into furniture manufacturing in 1970 according to figures provided by the National Forest Products Association from U. S. Forest Service publications. Pallets rather than crates use a lot. Fork-lift pallets (those cratelike affairs onto which various materials are stacked for warehousing as well as shipment, stabbed and lifted for loading by the zippy little fork-lift trucks) aren't all alike. Some are built for re-use but a lot of them become rubbish once they've reached their destination. Seek out local manufacturing and processing

15

plants which receive continuous shipments of materials on such pallets, and you will have a ready, continuing supply.

A few producers still ship edibles in wooden containers, some of which smell good and some of which can never be housebroken. Check with local restaurants, wholesalers and food processing houses. Local factories often get heavy machinery in good crates, so be on the lookout for expanding facilities notices in your local paper. Machine shops, certain automotive parts warehouses, an occasional plumbing supply house and perhaps other local enterprises will have a really good wooden box once in a while. Though it seems that most domestically manufactured items are packed in corrugated cartons with plastic fill or shipped in re-usable wooden containers if necessary, there are still some wood crates to be found.

Even crates not meant for re-use are often recycled by the local shop, so you cannot always secure what does exist. For instance, our local glass shop rebuilds the crates in which they receive bulk shipments of glass from the manufacturer to provide crating for their own special jobs.

The best source we've found is the wood and wood products used to provide a rigid framework within the corrugated cartons protecting some furniture and large musical instruments. You get an occasional sheet of very thin plywood this way too, and lighter sticks of various types.

Don't overlook your local retailers, including liquor stores and various outlets specializing in imported stuff. Find out which day their refuse is picked up and get there first. Some store owners will even call you when they've saved up some crates for you. Come running when they do and cart off all they want to get rid of. You're not required to use it all, and you'll keep them happy. Ask everyone. Antique dealers are one source of exotic crates from overseas, and undertakers get coffins in fine crates.

One of the all-time best end-use places to look is a building site. You are apt to find pallets and perhaps an odd crate or two considered as just so much rubbish along with all sorts of construction scraps. The use of lumber in residential housing accounts for four times the amount used in furniture manufacturing. Most building methods used today still leave considerable on-the-job waste. Even renovation jobs and nonresidential building use enough lumber to matter. On any building site, timing is important. What's available will vary with the stage of construction. You may find a few pallets from masonry materials shipments first, along with structural lumber scraps and construction-grade plywood. When the house is framed out, more plywood and structural lumber appear, followed by shingles or clapboards or other exterior siding and roofing, with or without pallets, as the house is closed in. Still later when the interior is being finished, look for flooring, paneling scraps and trim. Some fixtures and equipment may arrive in crates you'll spot long before they become available to you. Speak up early and plan to revisit often.

The best procedure on a building site is to find the construction superintendent. Make yourself known and be ready when the time comes to cart off what you can use. Since dumps are rapidly becoming sanitary landfills with rules about scavenging, it is important to skim the cream before the rubbish gets trundled off. Do watch it with the renovations, though. There is a market for used woodwork from period houses. You can't get for nothing what some salvage firm is paying for.

You'll find your scrounging skills grow with experience. Always ask permission and take only what is offered. The details will vary from one place to another, one time to another. Remember, once rubbish has been gathered up, the owner doesn't want to have to go pick it all up again, so leave the area neat when you finish choosing what you want. Towns that have sidewalk trash pickup in the business area often have ordinances about scavenging, littering, etc. It's really best to ask beforehand whether what you want is labeled "trash," but however you operate, you'll develop a scrounging technique that works well for you.

WHAT YOU'LL FIND

Nowhere is the garbage exactly the same. Sooner or later you are apt to find almost anything. In crates, pallets or construction scrap, there'll be solid wood, plywood, hardboard and perhaps chipboard, all products to consider for building the pieces suggested here. The bulk of your booty is apt to be solid wood of one species or another (that is, from one kind of a tree or another). You will find various sizes and shapes and also pieces in different stages of processing.

There are some stock lumber sizes with which you'll want to become familiar, particularly should you need to visit your local lumberyard. Dimension lumber starts out at the sawmill in even-inch sizes — 2x4, 2x6, 4x4, for example; boards measure 1x4, 1x6, 1x8, etc. But such nominal sizes diminish during the finishing processes. Industry standards provide that a 2x4, for instance, must measure not less than 1⅝" thick by 3⅝" wide even in S4S (sanded smooth on all four sides). Dimension lumber is referred to by its nominal size, but you know it will actually measure ¼" to ½" less. You may run across some full-thick or rough-cut boards that prove to be the full nominal size in crates or pallets, but don't count on it.

Lumber is also graded for quality according to industry specifications: straightness of grain, number of knots (and whether they are solid knots or knotholes), splits and checks and moisture content are all considered. Top-quality lumber is clear, even-grained with only solid knots, if any, square and straight-cut, kiln dried so there are no appreciable splits or checks. While the rules vary in detail from one species to another, obviously No. 2 simply does not meet the criteria as well as No. 1 grade does. The aim, of course, is to provide a consistent product, identified by a uniform labeling system. Actually, the very things that make a particular piece of wood less desirable as a product may make it extremely desirable in your eyes as a decorator piece.

Trim stock comes under a different set of industry standards; wood flooring, cedar shingles and shakes, etc. each have their own specifications. But the intent of each is similar — to insure a consistent product.

Trim of course also has stock profiles (shapes) to follow. In the rubbish at a job site will be short lengths of such stock and once in a while an 8" strip cut off the edge of a casing or a baseboard. These bits and pieces (generally softwood) often prove invaluable when you are really into making things.

You will not find that crates or pallets necessarily use lumber meeting these industry standards. The box factory is often an offshoot of the sawmill and can use odd pieces in its products to advantage. You will find box factories in every section of the country converting local woods into containers; consequently, a wide variety of species turns up. In general, the thinner, rough box woods will not be of much value to you in making furniture such as we show here. You need heavier stock, around ¾" thick. There's not much of that in orange crates and berry boxes. In fact, there aren't many wooden orange crates and berry boxes anymore.

Shipping crates from overseas often have interesting stencils and tags and labels affixed that you may want to preserve for their decorative value, but the wood they're painted on or stuck to may well be the splinteriest, roughest sort you've ever encountered. On the other hand, the Southern yellow pine that seems to be a favorite of the furniture craters may be fairly smooth, though not necessarily straight or flat. Some, used as a platform within a corrugated carton, is downright superlative for the purposes outlined in this book. And some of the pieces we found are actually SPIB No. 2 1x3 and 1x4 boards. (That is, they meet the Southern Pine Industry Bureau standards for No. 2 grade yellow pine in quality and size.)

On the West Coast, softwoods are used to make pallets, about 80 per cent using standard 1x6 boards, according to the National Wooden Pallet and Container Association. On the Eastern seaboard, pallets run more to full-thick 1x4's of local hardwoods, heavy in weight and hard to work but often attractive. Then, too, a lot of pallets are made to specification for a particular shipper, and they can run to widely variant sizes.

Wood that's been left lying outdoors may have weathered to a delightful silvery grey tone or it may show a greenish tinge due to the preservative used to treat the wood. This color can be painted over, but it won't take a good stain. Some wood may be green, not green in color but green in time — just-cut, undried lumber. Build with green wood and as it dries it shrinks, leaving loose joints and wider spaces than you intended. You may also find pieces from the perimeter of the log, even pieces with bark. Generally in the designs in this book, anything this irregular will not work well. That goes for excessively warped or twisted boards, too. You'll have to look further and be selective where you use what.

Plywood is wood, too, though its layers are built up of wood generally "peeled" from the log rather than cut from it. It gains its primary strength from the alternating direction of the grain from one layer to the next. Plywood scraps from construction may be ¼" to 1" or more thick of any quality, including hardwood-surfaced paneling. There are American Plywood Association specifications for various types. Plywood used in crates is apt to be very thin, possibly delaminating (glue failing to hold the layers of wood together) and may be of strange construction. You'll have to take a good look at what you find. In some of the projects that follow, thin, flat pieces of plywood can be substituted for planking.

This advice applies to hardboard, too. Some interior paneling is really hardboard with the "woodgrain" printed or embossed on it. Certain types of hardboard are used as underlayment, too. If you can find enough to use, hardboard ¼" thick can be used where you might otherwise use plywood. Thinner pieces of hardboard, ⅛" or so, make good drawer bottoms, as does much thin plywood. Hardboard can be cut for spacers and shims, so don't ignore it. You'll find it comes in very handy.

Chipboards or flakeboards you can recognize by their appearance. They look like a lot of large-grain sawdust or wood shavings squashed down flat, and unfortunately some types are not much more useful. The best suggestion here is to give a typical sample the hammer test. See how easily it breaks. If it passes that test, you can make use of it in about the same ways you would use plywood of a similar thickness.

Who knows what else you can find — wallboard scraps, floor tile, plastic, hardware, fabric, metal. You name it, sooner or later you'll find it, and who's to say you won't find a use for it. Floor tile to surface your table top is an obvious possibility, plastic for your lamps might be a consideration. Don't ignore it if you see a glimmer of possible use. It won't be there when you go back if you take time out to think about it.

SO YOU'VE FOUND IT, NOW WHAT?

There you are in front of a pile of crates, a few construction scraps and four nicely weathered pallets. The nice man said you can have it all, just take it away now.

Hopefully you've come prepared with wrecking bar or nail bar to take apart quickly the packing crate that obviously will not go in the back seat of your compact. Actually, if he's been saving crates for you, the store owner may well have flattened them already. He had to stack them in the least amount of space, didn't he? But he may have broken them and there are sure to be nails sticking out, so beware. Some scavenging is best done in gloves sturdy enough to deflect splinters at least.

You'll also have with you a few carpet scraps to line your truck, wagon or car, and time enough to remove the

more obvious sticking-straight-out nails or a hammer to turn them down with. At least make an effort to save most of the upholstery and the ceiling lining of your conveyance. It's up to you to bring the rope and pads if you intend to carry things on top of your car. Bring a red rag and a tack and hammer in case you get any long pieces you need to flag.

Pay attention to how you stack and pack to get the most into the space you do have. Stacking face to face and cleatside to cleatside allows you to stagger open-cleated units so they take up less height. East Coast pallets are heavy. Try to get them on the bottom in a station wagon so you needn't lift so high, though broken ones that can throw the pile off should go in later. Remember, you also have to see out the back well enough to drive safely. Make two trips if necessary.

Finding a "place" may well be your biggest problem. You need an area for disassembly as well as one for storage in addition to a place to construct and finish pieces. If you live in a house, you'll probably plan to do most of your work in the basement, garage or carport, but if you're an apartment dweller you may have a complication. You can carry bundles of lumber upstairs in the elevator much easier than you can move stacks of pallets around and with far fewer splinters, too. Inspecting each piece of wood for protruding nails, broken staples, tag ends of metal banding, etc. is a lot simpler than dragging a too-heavy-to-lift crate across the floor and maybe leaving a nasty gouge behind. If the superintendent won't let you use a corner of the basement, work outdoors. In some seasons that is the best answer for the disassembly stage anyhow. Do get a heavy duty extension cord for your basic equipment before you start.

Scraps from a building site are generally nice "new" wood requiring little work. But concrete spatters, caulking dribbles or, later, paint spills, may have rendered some pieces useless for your purposes. Seldom is it worthwhile to attempt to remove some unidentified sticky substance clinging to a few of your finds. It is better to toss them away. Even the tossing can turn into a problem. Remember, now it is up to you to get rid of the bits and pieces you can't use.

Crates and pallets are another matter. Reclaiming sound wood from such used constructions is not what you'd call an exact science. There are some principles that can be applied to advantage: (1) retrieve only what is useful, and (2) understand your adversary. First of all, when you have no means available to plane the wood down to a usable thickness, there is little to be gained by carefully taking apart a pallet to salvage the 1½" rock hard maple stringers which aren't straight or smooth anyhow. You would be better off to sacrifice the stringers to get the decking boards off intact if you can use them, even if it means buying a hacksaw blade and cutting the nails. So to start with, decide what pieces you want most to salvage. You might even go a step further and decide that the time/money equation works out to your greatest advantage if you buy a piece or more of wood at your local lumberyard. Actually, all the furniture pieces in this book could be duplicated in No. 2 yellow pine or equal grade wood for well under $400 even at today's prices. Or you could spend well over $1,500 to build the same pieces in cherry or walnut. It's up to you to figure out the fair make or break point on your labor time versus your cash outlay.

UNCONSTRUCTION AND DISASSEMBLY

It is possible that once in a great while you'll find a well-built crate you'll want to salvage intact. Possible but not likely, though hatch covers from navy surplus were advertised for sale not too long ago. Should you come across a well-made table-top-to-be, check it out for obvious splinters and protruding nails and get back to the business of salvaging boards for your lumber supply.

Consider the adversaries you'll meet in the disassembly business. Nails were invented as a much easier way of fastening together pieces of wood than fitting an interlocking joint or using a screw. Nails come in various styles. The common box nail has a relatively large, flat head and

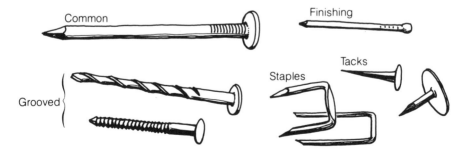

straight shank. If you can get under the head, you can lift these nails out with the claw end of a carpenter's hammer. Digging around on the face of the board you want in order to get under the nail head is not the way to do it.

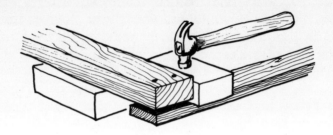

If you can get at the back of the board that the nails go through, try hammering on a block of wood placed close alongside the piece the nails go into. Use a scrap of wood at least as wide as the wood you are trying to get off. Don't hammer directly on the board you want or you'll probably split it. You have to support the whole construction in such a way that the board you are trying to remove has a place to go to if you are successful. With luck, hammering on the block will force the board you want, nails and all, away from the board you don't want. When it has lifted ¼" or so, turn the whole assembly over and try knocking the board back down. The nail heads should then be up, free of the board, so they can be pulled out.

Knowing the right way to use the claw end of your carpenter's hammer is the biggest how-to trick going for you. The basic mechanical principle behind all your "lifting" tools is that of the lever. It is like a teeter-totter. A heavy weight on a short arm from the center pivot (the fulcrum) can be moved by a very light weight at the end of the long arm. A hammer simply puts the long arm of the teeter-totter where you can grip it effectively.

There is a very tiny ledge at the bottom of the "V" between the claws which has to be got under the head of the nail. When you've engaged the nail head in the claws,

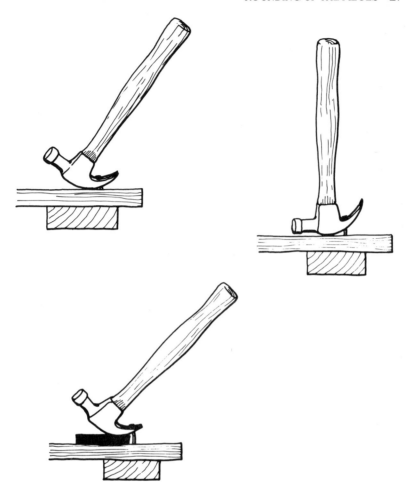

"roll" the hammer on the curve to the head. When the hammer handle is nearly vertical, the leverage designed into it is almost used up. Then you need to block under the head again and repeat the nail-pulling roll move. On easily marred wood, it's a good idea to use a scrap of hardboard under the hammer head throughout the process to save the surface.

If, when you knocked the board back down, the nails went back down too, it may still be possible to get the board off. Use the hammer-on-the-block method on the backside of the piece nailed through, moving the block around to free the whole piece. That is, lift the board with the nails a bit at each place it is nailed until the whole strip, nails and all, is free.

But don't stop. The nails still must be removed from the board. Any time you have occasion to hammer on the nail points to push the heads up, remember to support the board close to the nails so you are not working off in space somewhere. Beware the other nails sticking through with their points exposed, ready to stab you, too. The safety rule to follow here is: **ALWAYS CLEAN OFF BOARDS AS SOON AS THEY ARE FREED.** Puncture wounds from stepped on nails are most unpleasant.

Box nails are easy. There are other possible nail encounters awaiting you that aren't quite so simple. The smaller-headed finishing or casing nail or a box nail with the head missing may not yield to pulling out by the claw-under-the-head method. Sometimes you can work the board off right over the nail heads by pounding on a block on the back of the board. Then pull the nails left in the nailed-into piece. Bend them down to "hook" over the claw if they won't come out any other way. Drive them all the way into the piece if you really don't want to use it.

Coated nails are another variety that don't pull out easily. They have a resin coating that melts with the friction of being driven into the wood and then sets. The result is almost a glued-in nail. Break the bond and you can usually extract the nail. One method that can be tried for bond-breaking is that of racking the piece you wish to disassemble. Tip it to rest on one edge and push so as to set up diagonal stress, then reverse the direction and push again, stressing the opposite diagonal. Incidentally, racking is a pretty good way to break up glue joints and generally loosen up the works.

Encounters with normal nails are made difficult if they've been clinched. Clinching is most apt to be done

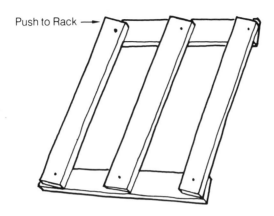

Push to Rack →

with common nails purposely selected too long for the pieces they unite. The excess is bent over on the backside and driven back into the wood from that direction. If the job has been well done, they are practically impossible to remove without considerable damage. Sometimes you can "dig out" the bent-over ends at the expense of that area of wood, declinch them, and drive them out from the back. Pounding once-bent nails out requires a bit of doing as they tend to rebend at the least mis-stroke. It is easier to get the heads clear, then pull them from the face side.

So much for regular nails. The next possibility, and one you are (unfortunately) very apt to run into, especially in pallets, is the grooved nail. In an effort to make better nails,

manufacturers have succeeded only too well with these fiendish developments. Annularly grooved nails have rings around the shank that become embedded in the wood fibers as the nail is driven in. Pulling these out, regardless of the type of head, is next to impossible.

Spirally grooved (helical) nails (they look like a stretched-out screw thread) are only a tiny bit easier. Once in a while they will "unscrew" as you pull them. Sometimes you can drive them on into the nailed-into piece using another nail to set them through, thus freeing the nailed-on piece. That is if the top piece is relatively thin. It is worth a try, if you can get at the back, to apply the hammer-on-the-block method of lifting the board off. With grooved nails, the board is apt to come off leaving the nails behind, immobile in the nailed-into piece. It also leaves oversize splintered holes in the piece removed. Unless you particularly want the piece the nails have stayed in, just drive them on in and discard it. Generally you will not be able to pull out these tenacious varieties without an awful lot of exertion.

If the block-on-the-back method has not been successful and you are determined to have that particular board and you can get a hacksaw blade between the nailed-on and the nailed-into pieces, you can saw through the nails. Hammer the stumps into the nailed-into wood. Drive the head sections out of the nailed-on piece and you've got it. Chances are, though, that if you can't pull the nails, you can't get the blade in to cut them. In that case you can still save some of the wood by sawing it free but **MAKE SURE YOU WILL NOT BE SAWING ANY NAILS OR OTHER METAL BY ACCIDENT.**

One specific possibility might be worth mentioning here. If you are trying to use pallets and have resorted to sawing the wood free, make the cuts along the inside of the two outside stringers, netting a sort of backbone with ribs attached — the center stringer with the decking boards still nailed to it. Support one board at a time on both sides of the stringer and try hammering down on the stringer. Some-

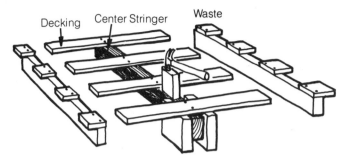

times this method will work. You'll have a board with two nail holes in the middle but a longer length than the two short sawed pieces would have been. It's worth a try. The two outside stringers with the short deck blocks remaining irrevocably nailed on aren't worth struggling with, but the center stringer, if freed, might be useable.

When mechanization hits the box factory, it often introduces peculiar styles of nail heads, but as a practical matter even these reduce to two kinds: those you can get a claw hammer under and those you can't. One other bit of mechanical innovation is the metal or sometimes plastic strapping you may find. Sometimes this is a simple strip of metal nailed on, more or less as reinforcement. Treat it as an enlarged nail head and try to lift it by working your "lifter" between the strap and the wood. Other times the metal strap is a tension device and will have been severed by the store owner to get the crate open. He has the right tool to cut the material. If you have to do it, try tin snips, or if the strap seems thicker, a hacksaw. The kind of strap with self-prongs usually has made such a mess of the wood under that area that prying it out is not worthwhile. Sawing out the damaged area, complete with pronged part still attached, is usually more satisfactory, though of course you can try lifting the whole strip with wrecking bar or jimmy. If the prongs are clinched, dig under the bent-down prongs first, then rip off the strap.

Once in a great while you will find a wood screw used. They generally react well to being unscrewed. On heavy crates, bolts and nuts are a possibility. If they are straight, re-use is possible. If they are rusted, use rust remover. If they are "frozen," try penetrating oil.

There is still another whole group of fasteners which we will call staples though there are various technical terms for specific designs. We found unclinched soft-wire staples in furniture carton frames, clinched flat-wire staples in some plywood cases, fence staples on a couple of wire-bound jobs and some smaller, broader staples fastening very thin wood to good, solid bases. And that is only a very tiny sample of the variety there is in this area.

In the case of an unclinched staple, if there is even a small loop above the face of the fastened-on board, you have a chance of pulling it out. What you really need is a one-clawed claw hammer but none has been brought to our attention. The jimmy is too wide and using only one claw of the hammer will tend to make a mark in the wood.

A substantial tack puller seems to be the best bet. More often, you'll have to separate the boards, thus exposing the two prongs of each staple. Driving the staple out by hammering on these projecting prongs is not as simple as it sounds. Hit one square and often you bend the other one more. Perfecting your hammer aim is the answer. Once the loop is raised, turn the board over and pull the staple, blocking up the tack puller as you did the claw hammer and for the same reason.

Clinched staples are twice as hard to remove as clinched nails, but attack them the same way. If it is the nailed-into piece you want, you can be a bit more destructive and pry out bits of wood from under the staple loop until there is room clear to lift the staple out. This process makes a splintery mess of the top piece but the stapled area was pretty well shot before anyway.

You've noticed we said "where you can get at the backside of the piece you want to remove." You can't always. Then you need your prying tools. Remember — these are destructive tools and your purpose is not to destroy but to salvage. Prying with a ½" wide jimmy against a 4" board you want will most likely result in a ½" wide section being split out. Use a wider floor chisel to make the initial separation. Even the various patented and unpatented prying wedge bars 1½" or 2" wide are better in

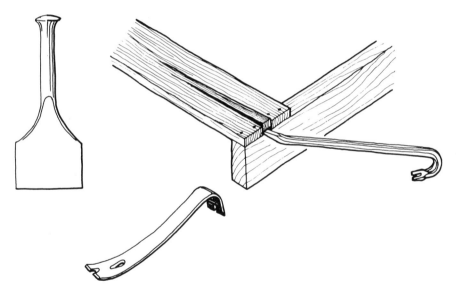

this case. True, you are going to need the heavier bars when you have to rip apart something solid to get at something you want, but do take it easy. A broken or split board is a wasted board. Lift under *all* the area and you strain across the grain. With too narrow a pry, you strain part of the wood *along* the grain where it promptly splits.

Understanding about the mechanic principle of the inclined plane wouldn't hurt. The plane transfers the power delivered to the end into push power off the angled face. If that face is narrow, the area being pushed is narrow. If the point of least resistance is the strength of the wood itself, it splits. The wedge principle combines two inclined planes back to back. Force delivered to the end is transferred into forces delivered off both angled faces.

The next obvious thing is that a crowbar, ripping bar, wrecking bar, pinch bar or jimmy combine at the pry end a wedge tip with a lever action curve. Think through how that combination is going to act before you tackle an 8' long board from the side with a wedge tip and then lever. Toothpicks come off. Take it easy and figure out how to make the tools you have work for you.

You can get most useable crate lumber free with a claw hammer (a ripping hammer is a bit better if you have both), a wide-bladed bar of some sort (a pry bar, a floor chisel, or a 2¾" wide electrician's chisel), some sort of wrecking bar with nail puller at one end and an angled

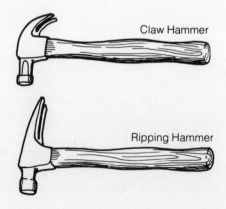

Claw Hammer

Ripping Hammer

wedge-pointed pry at the other, and a sturdy tack lifter. Such are the Tools of Destruction. But having the proper tools is not enough. You have to use common sense. Check, whenever you are about to insert and use any pry, where the other end is going if your prying works all at once (it is to be hoped not into your shoulder) and where the piece being pried off is going to fall.

As we said, this work is not an exact science. Canvas work gloves are a help simply in handling crate wood before you de-nail it and as you stack it to size for inventory. Eliminate the possibility of puncture wounds by always cleaning up projecting nails and other sharp points immediately, and lessen the chance for rips and scratches by using your head. Using your feet is sometimes the answer to holding down one piece while you lift off another. Propping up two parts free of the floor while you force off the underneath cross tie is one way to prevent the sort of disaster a recklessly loosened cleat coming towards you can cause. Think first.

GETTING IT ALL TOGETHER

Once you've got a stockpile of lumber ready, you're probably going to be anxious to start putting a few of them together. But please, read the whole book first.

THE TOOLS YOU'LL NEED

To put things together, you will need some tools. Exactly which tools you'll select will be up to you. We could make a list of the absolutely best tool for performing each task needed to construct the projects that follow, but that would not necessarily reflect the best choice for your over-all situation.

Some of the same tools you used for destruction may be used for construction. If you are totally unequipped you'll want to buy the best you can afford and take care of them properly. Scheduling your purchases rather than buying everything at once on time may make the best sense with your budget. If you're in a make-do setup, that's another story. Often you'll find you have some of the tools we're going to discuss but need others. Our suggestion is to read the whole book first and see what applies to your own situation and when. It may well be that tool rental is the solution for you if your schedule permits you to take advantage of it.

The person who wants to build up a basement workshop full of tools will make different selections from someone who just wants to make some furniture quickly, easily and inexpensively. The furniture in this book is designed to be built with a minimum number of tools and with an eye to finances. That is, power tools are nice but if you can't afford them, you can still build furniture. If you have or can get certain power tools, we have a couple of suggestions as to which will prove most useful for these projects.

Measure and Mark

First you'll need measuring and marking tools. A try square will permit you to test the squareness of a board and provide a guide for marking your sawcuts at right angles to the edge. A combination square with removable blade will do all that and can be used as a marking gauge and as a level (if it has a bubble level built into the frame). With the slide-out rule the combination square allows you to set and transfer measurements from one place to another. You can get by with a try square and a ruler, but the combination square is a better buy.

A 25' or longer steel tape, which you'll need for longer measurements, will also come in handy in measuring your rooms for carpeting, tile and draperies and to see if the furniture will fit. The style with the square-based case makes it easier to take inside measurements by adding the length of the case (it will say what factor that is on the case) to the dimension read from the tape. There are times when you'll wish you had a carpenter's square with its 24" blade, especially for scribing long lines at right angles to one edge.

The accurate way to mark is with a steel scriber, or scratch awl. The way to mark so you can see it is with a pencil. A chisel point is more accurate than a pencil-sharpener point but either way, do keep the pencil sharp. Use a different pencil for the figuring you'll have to do and get yourself a scratch pad to do the figuring on.

Sawhorses or Workbenches

With a measuring device at hand, you could start to work on a sturdy kitchen table. But sooner or later you are going to want something to saw on and a place to put the parts while the glue sets. We strongly suggest that two pairs of sawhorse brackets will pay for themselves many times over. These devices allow you to convert simple lengths of 2x4 into rugged sawhorses capable of support- ing almost anything: the cabinet door you use as a work

Sawhorse
Brackets

surface, the two planks you make do with, two 2x8s you use as a scaffolding to paint the ceiling from, a piece of plywood you eventually invest in for a larger table top, three light planks you use as a wallpapering table, the strips you dry your wash on when the dryer breaks, the roof structure when your kids want to play house, and goodness knows what else. In short, sawhorses come in handy. You'll need them first for sawing. Set them up with the top bars parallel, far enough apart to support fully the long end of the board you wish to cut, with the saw line usually about a hand's width beyond the right-hand horse. With short boards, offset the horses to get the proper distance apart, of course.

Naturally, if you already have a workshop with a good bench, you really don't need horses, though they are still pretty handy to have around. One way or another, you do need a flat, level area to work on and a good light to see by.

Saws of All Sorts

Sawhorses bring us to considering the saw or saws you'll need for these projects. You can make do with a crosscut saw if you've been able to find a variety of board widths that require no ripping. (Crosscutting is, obviously, cutting across the grain, as you would in cutting a long log up into shorter sections. Ripping is cutting with the grain as is done in the sawmill in making boards out of the long logs.) If a hand saw is your choice (there is a lot of sawing to be done and power makes it easier and faster) you'll want maybe not the best available but close to it. Eight points to the inch (that's how they count the teeth of the saw) in the 26" length is the most popular. You do not want a toy nor do you want one so cheap it won't stay sharp. If you already have an old saw, perhaps it would be worthwhile to clean off the rust (use a rust remover) and have it set and sharpened for you.

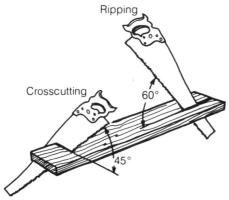

If you have or plan a full-scale basement workshop you'll eventually invest in a circular table saw or a radial arm saw. Access now to either would be great for making these pieces but such an investment to build this furniture is not realistic. If you do plan to buy, select the model and type in terms of your overall needs. Either of these power saws will greatly simplify making the pieces in this book.

On the other hand, perhaps you are gung ho to build your own house or undertake other major construction outside the workshop. You will undoubtedly want to consider a portable circular saw. It too will greatly simplify building these pieces, but the price is not really justified just to build the furniture. To build furniture and remodel the attic, a portable saw would most likely be a justified expense.

Saber Saw

The least expensive of the power saws generally is a saber saw, a handy, easily handled and very adaptable mechanism that will do the job at hand adequately and which you'll find yourself using often. Even if you eventually have a table saw or a portable circular saw, there will

Portable Circular Saw
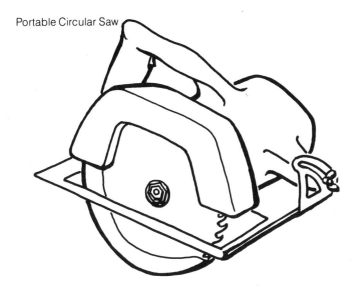

still be times you want a saber saw. For instance, it is difficult to cut the hole for an electrical outlet in a 4x8 sheet of paneling with anything other than a saber saw. If you've never used power tools before, there is something confidence-building about learning to handle the saber saw that makes it a good choice here.

With any power tool, there are precautions. The most obvious one of course is **DON'T CUT THE WIRE**. Even that requires a little forethought. Arrange your work area so the tool plugs in where the cord will (1) not get in the way as you cut; (2) not get in your way as you move around; and (3) reach to the far end of the work you plan to do. Many of the tools marketed today are double-insulated so the danger of shock from the tool is eliminated. If yours isn't, that third prong on the plug is there to ground the tool. If you are plugging into a grounded outlet (one with a place for the third prong), no worry. If you must use an adapter, then put the wire from the adapter properly under the screw that holds the works in place so that you have in fact created a grounded outlet. Last thing, before you plug it in, **MAKE SURE THE TOOL IS SWITCHED OFF**. There is nothing so upsetting as an unattended power tool roaring at you from the quiet place you set it before you turned your back to plug it in. Whichever power tools you buy, do insist on the manufacturer's manual which will give you information on use and maintenance care. Many companies also offer additional literature for sale that will help you see what else the tool you've bought is capable of doing.

What you want your saw to do right now is cut straight along the line you've marked and, most important, perpendicularly straight from the face of the wood you're cutting. That means you not only have to align the direction of cut with the line you drew, but you also have to hold the saw so the blade makes a truly perpendicular cut. With a handsaw, you'll find your position has a lot to do with it. With a table saw or a radial arm saw you push the wood on the table past the sawblade, blade and table being held in the 90° relationship you desire; it is practically impossible to goof. With portable saws you are in between. Both a circular saw and a saber saw are made with a shoe that is at right angles to the blade but it is up to you to see that the shoe rests fully on the board you are cutting. A circular saw is generally heavy enough to settle itself pretty well but it is easy to ride a saber saw along cockeyed on one edge of the shoe if you don't get the feel of it right in the first place. Practice. Cutting straight with a circular saw is easier than with a saber saw. You have the better part of the circular blade to fit into the kerf you've cut as you go. Deviate from the straight ahead and you'll feel the blade bind. The narrow saber saw gives you no such warning. You may find it helpful to tack or clamp on a guide strip for the edge of the shoe to run against to keep the cut straight and where you want it. Just make sure you don't let the shoe slip under the guide strip, and keep the clamps out of the blade's path.

Ripping with a table or radial arm saw is simple provided you use the proper blade. With a circular saw, the combination blade will usually do a passable job, but take care in how you support the board you wish to make narrower. With a saber saw, ripping is possible but difficult. Try to avoid it. The lighter weight saw tends to follow the grain rather than the line you've marked. Allow excess for bringing the edge down level by other means.

Shaping and Smoothing

Those "other means" are not necessarily traditional wood planes. One of the best tools invented is a series of tools the Stanley Company came up with a few years ago.

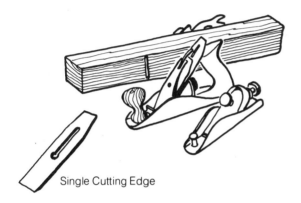

Single Cutting Edge

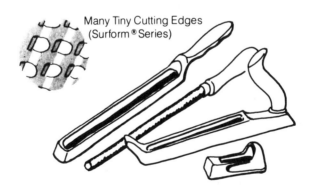

Many Tiny Cutting Edges
(Surform® Series)

The Surform® series acts fast, like many tiny planes, cutting off the rough surface and corners of shaggy wood, giving shape and final fit to otherwise impossible materials. The tools all use a perforated and sharpened Sheffield steel material on the business surface. Differing shapes and sizes are mounted in appropriate handles and frames. There is a long file shape that is the most reasonable in price, though the large plane is perhaps easier to control on the long straight edges you will be most concerned with. For going across end grain to smooth up that sloppy saw-cut, either of those shapes will work, or the shorter block plane style will be effective. These tools are held flat to the surface of the work but the angle at which they are pushed across it can be varied somewhat to provide the desired cutting action. If you don't have a saber saw, do have the round file (⅜") in addition to one of the flat ones. Replacement blades are available.

Smoothing It Out

Even the order in which you buy tools is subject to considerable variation. If you've found nothing but splintery wood, you should have got the Surform tools first, used them and then sanded piece by piece before you stacked your raw materials. No point in picking and choosing from splintery boards you'll have to smooth before use anyhow. Sooner or later you will want to examine each board carefully for loose knots, straightness, warp, splits and splinters as well as appearance. Stack your raw materials according to the size of the cross section first, keeping all boards of the same thickness together, then worry about the lengths you have available. You may have found full-sized 1x4 rough-sawed lumber. That will work as well as the S4S finish stock you'd buy in the lumber yard *except* that it is rough. That means you need something to sand with right now.

If you are building only one piece of furniture, you can probably get by working by hand with a piece of coarse sandpaper over a wood block followed by a bit of medium grit. For a whole room full of furniture you are going to want to use one of those newfangled inventions: a power sander.

For the kind of work you'll be doing here, the ¼" drill attachment is one possibility if you already have the ¼" drill. For the workshop person, a faceplate with sanding disc would get a real workout in smoothing out crate lumber. For the apartment dweller and the average homefixer, an oscillating pad sander is the most reasonable buy, though the work required here can be done with a belt sander. The belt sander will do a lot of the rougher work faster but it is really a more heavy-duty piece of portable equipment with a correspondingly higher heavy-duty price. The most logical middle-range choice remains a reasonably good oscillating sander, preferably one with the optional switch for straight-ahead sanding. Visit your local hardware or tool center and check out the features on the various models in the price range you like. There is some

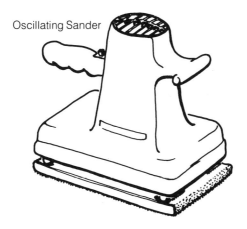

Oscillating Sander

variation in weight, ease of changing paper, wiring (double-insulated or three-wired), switch positioning, etc. that may lead you to favor one make over another. As with all tool purchases, question the value of each special feature extolled to you. Just why is that particular feature of advantage to *you*?

Noise

A special consideration, particularly for apartment dwellers, is the noise produced by all this activity. If you're out in the boonies, the screeching sound of a reluctant nail being pulled hardly matters. If you're on the other side of a flimsy partition after midnight it can be quite annoying. It helps to work on a thick pad of newspapers for your cutting and pulling earlier on, saving things like Surform and hand sanding for later — they're quieter. Power sanding is comparable to a heavy-duty vacuum cleaner which you also wouldn't run after eleven p.m. or so. The whine of a power saw doesn't go unnoticed either. Where you live, how well you get on with your neighbors and what time of day or night it is will all have some bearing on what you do when with what.

Tools for Making Fasteners Fasten

By now you want to put boards together. You'll need a good hammer. A rock in the hand will drive nails but you've only the length of your arm to add force. With a hammer you have the weight of the head at the end of an "arm extension" to do part of the work for you and you have the resiliency of the handle to absorb part of the shock.

No toys; you want a carpenter's claw hammer. Heft a few. Get one that you find comfortable. There is not much point in buying the 16-ounce one if you have trouble controlling a 13-ounce. Make the hammer work for you. When you want a tiny tap to start a nail, it's fair to "choke" the hammer (hold it near the head), but when you want the most pounds delivered to the nail head, get the most out of your hammer by gripping it comfortably at the handle end and swinging as if you meant it.

The face of the hammer will eventually come in contact

with the wood as you drive the nail home. If it is really wrecked, you will see the damage. If you've bought a new hammer, save it from this sort of destructive treatment by using a wood block between it and the end of your chisel or wedge in the disassembly stages.

A hammer is another of those tools where quality features run up the price. At least spend enough to get a forged head rather than a cast one, but try not to pay a premium for fancy grips you don't really need. You can drive a few tacks with a too-large hammer but you can't hammer 6d nails with a tack hammer. Know what you need and shop until you find it. More about hammering under fasteners.

Related to fasteners in this group of furniture pieces is the occasional need to drill holes. Again, power is nice if you can afford it. A ¼" drill, if you already have one, will make short work of drilling the few holes required. Buying a ¼" drill just for the drilling involved in making every piece in this book is probably not worth it. In any case, study the price tags carefully and make the compromise that makes the most sense to you. There are several possible combinations. A hand drill will do the necessary drilling for the screws and bolts required and attach the hardware shown for the major furniture pieces. It will not take the 1" bit required for the tool tote's wooden dowel handle. If you haven't a friend with an auger bit and brace, consider screwing in a dowel cut to fit between the tote ends as an alternate. The clearance holes for assembling the two lamps as shown also require a drill larger than will fit into a ¼" chuck hand drill normally. Here there are three possible outs: (1) see your friend with the $^7/_{16}$" auger bit and brace again; (2) get a spade bit with a straight shank meant for a ¼" power drill; it will be extremely hard going in a hand drill but, in all except the hardest wood, it will work; or (3) rent a power drill, planning all your drilling jobs together to make it worthwhile. Considering future use, too, you may decide to purchase a good power drill. As with the

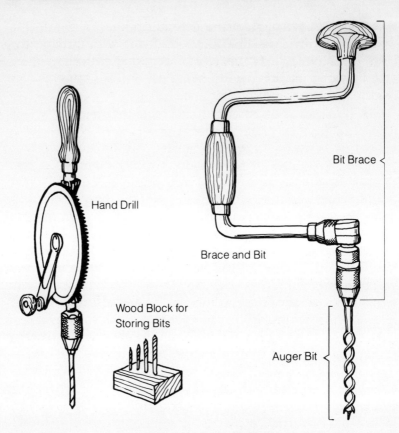

Hand Drill

Bit Brace

Brace and Bit

Wood Block for
Storing Bits

Auger Bit

other tools, evaluate the features of different models carefully. Stick with a well-known brand name and beware overloaded drill-and-accessories package deals. Do you need those accessories?

A hand drill is all you really need to make the furniture properly. Buy a reasonably good one, ¼" chuck capacity. You'll need a ¼" bit for wood and one or two smaller sizes for pilot holes for the screws to attach hardware. You may also want a drill to countersink for a 1½" x #8 or a 2" x #10 flathead wood screw. Unless you can persuade someone to gift you with a full set of drill bits, buy them as you buy your hardware in just the sizes you require. Drill a wood block to store them in.

You will of course need screwdrivers. Buy them sized to the screws you wish to drive and reserve them for driving. Don't use them for prying open paint cans, unsticking windows or chipping up floor tiles. Again, quality costs more. More about driving screws later.

Extra Hands

One of the handiest gadgets invented is the "C" clamp. It is so handy one tends to use it where another type of clamp might be better, but for doing double duty, "C" clamps are the most adaptable. You will have occasion to use bar or pipe clamps to advantage (in edge-to-edge gluing of tabletops, case tops and doors). An accomplished cabinetmaker would probably prefer screw-type furniture clamps to build up certain other parts. We have designed these pieces with glue-nail joints which won't give you the super-pro job properly glued and clamped joints will, but you aren't working with super-pro wood either. If you plan

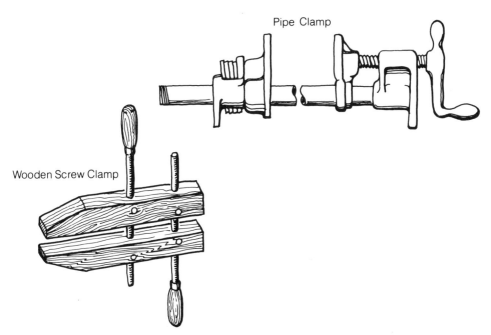

Pipe Clamp

Wooden Screw Clamp

to do a lot of furniture work, you'll probably want to invest in and learn how to use effectively wooden screw clamps as well as bar clamps, but neither is necessary for the tasks outlined here.

C Clamp

Four-inch and six-inch "C" clamps, ideally one pair in each size, will see you through clamping a guide strip for trimming your battened table top or door assembly with a saber saw, holding cleats in place while you check locations and nail or drill for bolts, holding chair seat to frame while you drill and countersink for screws, etc. Also use them to hold your extension cord out of the way (don't clamp onto it, just thread it through the "C"), use them to measure off your macrame cord for seats, etc. But always use a scrap of wood under the jaws to prevent marring the parts clamped.

When it comes to making the lamps and lantern shown, you will need a pair of pliers as well as the right

Needle-Nose Pliers

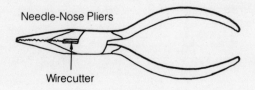

Wirecutter

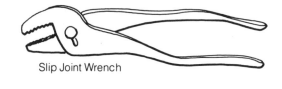

Slip Joint Wrench

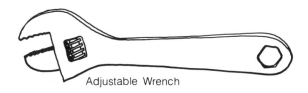

Adjustable Wrench

size screwdriver. The all-round-home-style needle-nose with wirecutter is probably as good a buy as any. Buy decent ones and remember pliers are for bending things, wrenches are for holding and tightening. You'll need a small, flat open-end wrench for the locknuts encountered in assembling the lighting pieces shown or, at the very least, an adjustable wrench small enough for the job. A knife that will strip insulation from the lamp cord is a necessity, too. These are all the sort of tools often found lurking in kitchen cabinet drawers, but never when the odd job they are really needed for is at hand. Check out your tool supply early on. Don't buy something you already have three of.

FASTENERS AND FASTENING

Nails and Hammering

You've selected your hammer. You've found out a few things about nails by taking things apart. To hold things together with nails you need to know what type and size nail to use, how many and where to put them and how to drive them where you want them. For the most part common nails (box nails) are available, drive easily, hold well enough, but don't look terribly attractive. Finishing nails with the tiny heads are available, drive almost as easily, hold almost as well and look a lot better. With glue, you certainly don't need common nails.

How many nails where has a few rules (which are not quite as strict if you use glue too) that will guide you well. First, nail across the grain rather than into end grain

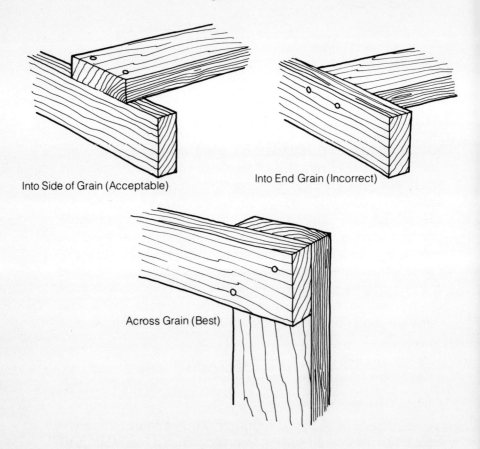

Into Side of Grain (Acceptable)

Into End Grain (Incorrect)

Across Grain (Best)

wherever you possibly can. Don't nail too close to the end of a board. Stagger your nailing pattern. If you are fastening a thin piece to a much thicker one, choose a nail three times as long as the thin board's thickness. Fastening two or more

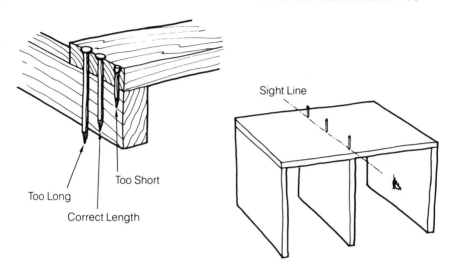

Too Long

Too Short

Correct Length

Sight Line

boards together should always take the longest nail possible without sticking through the last board. Nails are stronger in shear than in tension, even better if they are angled.

With a glue-nail joint, you are not relying on the holding power of the nail entirely but rather on its holding the parts together while the glue sets. Consequently while end grain is still to be avoided, the glue will hold in that surface too. Nails need not be quite as long either. It is best to start all the nails in the nailed-on piece, apply your glue and then set the piece in position carefully and complete the nailing.

You can see where to nail if you'll look at the end or edge of the pieces you wish to fasten together. Sight along the meeting edges to align the nails' positions. Wherever possible let the nail heads be on the inside of the piece where they will not show as much (if both pieces are the same thickness and you have a choice in the matter). We try to suggest in the project drawings both an approximate number and a reasonable nailing pattern, but requirements will vary somewhat as you may not be using exactly the same size of wood we were.

Nails are useful in non-fastening jobs too. If you don't have an awl, you can use a nail to start screws with.

If, in spite of having selected a reasonable size nail, the wood constantly splits when you try to drive it, try reversing the nail on a hard surface, give the pointed end a couple of taps, and try nailing again.

Screws and Screw Driving

We used two types of threaded fasteners in building these pieces. Flathead wood screws are the more typical of the two. Available in a number of different metals and finishes, they come in numbered sizes and different lengths. To work well in most woods wood screws require that a pilot hole somewhat smaller in diameter than the threaded portion be drilled in the screwed-into piece. If you are working with hardwood the clearance hole in the fastened-on piece can be almost as large as the un-threaded part of the screw. In softwoods, make it a bit smaller. The flathead screw should have a proper counter-sink (the beveled circle for the underside of the screw head to fit into). The easiest way to provide a pilot hole, clear-ance hole and countersink is to use a drill-bit-like affair made especially for the purpose. You will need one for

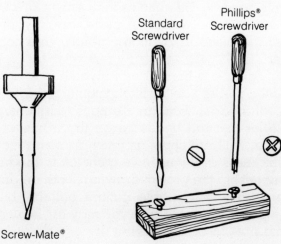

Screw-Mate®

Standard Screwdriver

Phillips® Screwdriver

each size and length of screw used. There is also an adjustable type which will accommodate screws of different lengths. Either kind can be used in a ¼″ chuck.

Screw heads come in two styles, slotted and cross-slotted (Phillips®). You need a screwdriver the proper size and the proper configuration for the screws you will use. The blade of a regular screwdriver is meant to fit rather closely in the slot to provide a good purchase for driving the screw. When you use a screwdriver indiscriminately for prying jobs and so on, it gets chewed up and either will not fit in the slot or tends to slip out and mess it up. An *old* screwdriver is a really good paint can opener but don't use it after that for driving screws. If the screws seem too hard to drive, try a little wax or soap on the threads.

A frequent use for screws is attaching hardware. In these projects we used packaged hinges and pulls that come with their own screws and bolts. Should you have occasion to purchase hardware and screws separately, you can identify the type of screw to use by the presence or lack of a countersink in the hardware. Ask for the length you want, measuring from the top of a flathead screw to the tip or from the underside of the head of round, pan or oval-headed screws.

Bolts and machine screws thread into metal rather than wood and the threads are consequently quite different in appearance from wood screw threads; also, the end is flat rather than pointed. We used machine screws with wing nuts to hold the chair and sofa together. A wing nut is tightened with the fingers while square or hexagonal nuts require wrenches. The slot in a machine screw allows you to hold it with a screwdriver but do get one with a blade wide enough to fit the size screw head you are using. Check the hardware you buy packaged, too. Often those machine screws will have cross-slotted heads which require a Phillips® screwdriver of the proper size. In soft wood, smaller diameter screws can be driven into a hole made by driving a nail partway in and then removing it.

Hold Bolt While Tightening Wing Nut

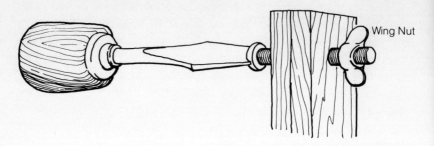

Wing Nut

Locate one screw and run it partway in first, then pilot-nail for the others. Work through the hardware to be attached, of course. Machine screws and bolts are not supposed to thread into the wood so you'll be drilling a clearance hole for such things as attaching handles and pulls. Use the size drill the manufacturer suggests. It will clear the threads and give you a bit of clearance without being too large.

Selecting the proper length of machine bolts and screws for use with a nut requires that you add the total thickness of the materials plus the height of the nut plus the thickness of any washer or lock washer you'll use plus ⅛″ to ¼″ to arrive at a standard length. Wood screws, on the other hand, should be selected so that the greater part of the threaded portion is in the fastened-into piece without the screw penetrating on out the back.

There are a couple of other bits of hardware you might like to consider for use in these projects. First, for quick, neat demountability and reassembly there are a number of patented inserts that put machine screw threads in wood so you can repeatedly bolt on and off. Each is available with the manufacturer's instructions for installation.

Another good idea is the pronged buttons that hammer into the bottom of things so they rest more easily on the floor. You might also want to investigate various types of furniture rests, glides and slides offered by the same mail order houses that carry threaded inserts.

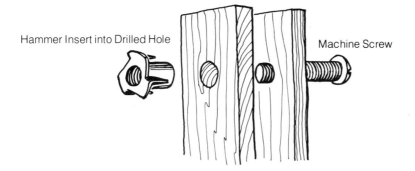

Hammer Insert into Drilled Hole   Machine Screw

Light chain and lid supports are other refinements you may want to consider (see toy chest and headboard specifics). Both are available by mail order if you cannot find them locally.

Glues and Clamping

The secrets of good gluing are (1) selecting a glue meant for the work you expect it to do; (2) applying it according to the manufacturer's directions; (3) holding the parts together and leaving them alone while the glue sets up; and (4) *wiping up excess immediately*. White glue can be used for the projects in this book. All polyvinyl white glues turn practically colorless when set up. Their drying time is about half an hour. Instead of white glue, you could use an aliphatic resin adhesive. It has some of the handling ease of white glue and the toughness of hide glue. If you want the the strongest possible glue bond, you might use a liquid hide glue. It allows more unhurried assembly as it takes over an hour to set up and twenty-four hours to reach a full-strength bond.

Whatever you use, try not to smear it around; even a little glue on the wood surface will show up when finishing time comes.

PUTTING EACH PART IN ITS PLACE

We said way back in the Introduction that building furnishings from crate lumber is creative, that you have to do some of the thinking that transforms the lumber you've scrounged into useful pieces for your home. You'll learn a lot by doing but you'll also learn to think it through first.

Take inventory of the stock at hand. You've sorted the lumber as you cleaned and stacked it away. Now you need to figure out where to use which piece. Board foot totals will do you no good. You want to know which boards the same thickness you can use together to make a table top and if you make it that big, which pieces will be left for the apron and legs. That sort of thinking is the only way to arrive at an intelligent plan of using the lumber you've accumulated. It's also the way to learn to see the possibilities in a given scrap heap.

There will be times when you realize it will be a long wait for thin plywood to turn up on the dump. It may be cheaper to buy hardboard for those drawer bottoms. Your time is worth something. That kind of evaluation can only be made by you, there, where you are. Studying the project diagrams will give you a good idea of what specific things to look for. Before you get too specific, a few generalities may be in order.

ILLUSTRATED GLOSSARY OF CONSTRUCTION TERMS

First, the glue-nailed *butt joint* requires accuracy of cut for good gluing into the end grain. You will want to check with your finger-tip—feel for flushness and double check with the combination square until you can "feel" when you have a butt joint cut squarely both ways.

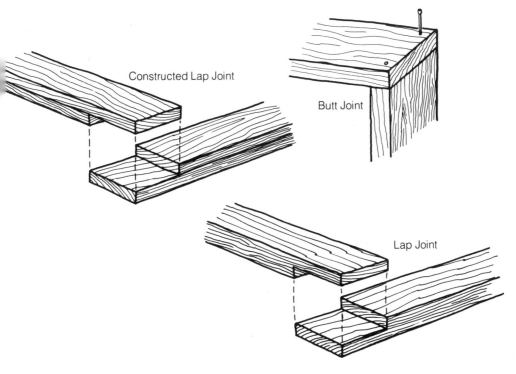

Constructed Lap Joint

Butt Joint

Lap Joint

Most of the major pieces shown utilize *constructed lap joints*. A *lap joint* in solid wood requires careful control of depth and width of cut in both members, careful measuring and careful surfacing. In constructed lap joints, care in selection of frame wood for the two parts of each piece will insure accuracy in forming the join, the width and depth of the lap being controlled by the finish size of the lumber being used. All you have to do is cut straight.

Another construction principle is the *batten*, which is any piece fastened across a series of parallel pieces. If it is under the parallel pieces and supports them evenly on its top surface, it is also a *cleat*. (But a cleat may support only a single piece, too.)

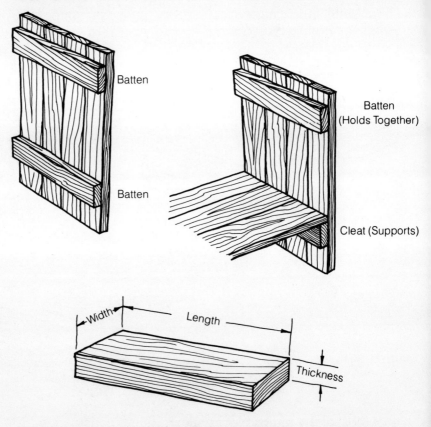

To clarify terms, make a note: in wood, the measurement with the grain is the *length*; the longer dimension across the grain the *width*; the shorter cross-grain measurement is the *thickness*.

In this book, a *plank* is a board, usually one of a series of similar pieces.

A *slat* is a smaller board, parallel to similar pieces but with space left between them.

We've chosen to call certain sub-assemblies by names descriptive of their construction. The same concept reappears again and again in the series. If we are successful here and in the project how-to information proper in conveying these concepts to you, you'll see immediately how simple it all really is and understand how to alter and adapt the designs to fit your needs.

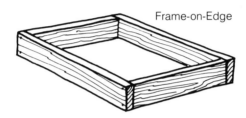

Frame-on-Edge

For instance, the *frame-on-edge* is a butt-joined rectangle formed of four boards the same width set on edge.

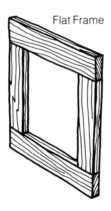

Flat Frame

A *flat frame* is four boards arranged in a rectangle but laid flat. It is seldom used as a separate structure but is a convenient term for describing that configuration.

Open Frame

The *open frame* is a pair of flat frames of the same size joined so the corners meet in a constructed lap joint as described.

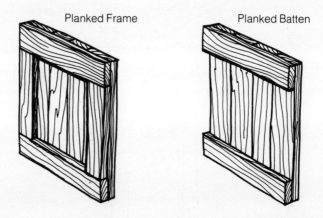

Planked Frame   Planked Batten

The *planked frame* actually consists of two battens flush with the top and bottom of a series of parallel planks and decorated with the two other members of a flat frame.

The *planked batten* is the same thing—undecorated.

You will soon see that the *apron* pieces under the table and desk tops and often the batten of a planked batten are joined at right angles to open or planked frames and form a frame-on-edge in the horizontal plane. Which gets us back to where we started.

GETTING DOWN TO SPECIFICS

Before you begin building, please read all the way through this book, at least all the way through the project section, at least all the way through the project section up to the project you want to build first. We've arranged the projects in a specific order so as to introduce one new concept at a time. We've tried not to repeat simplistic instructions over and over. If you didn't really *learn* the procedure the first time, you'll need to refer to the basic how-to when the same method is used in a later project. With this learn-as-you-go approach, you'll be a good rough carpenter by Project 22. Go to it.

Project 1

(Color Plate 1)

PLANT BOX

Select a board for the Bottom about ¾" thick and between 12" and 24" long. Use whatever width board will make a box wide enough for a few of your potted plants and their saucers to stand in. The board you use for Sides and Ends can be thinner and nominally 4", 6" or even 8" wide.

1-1. Reread the *Measure and Mark* section. Check that one end of the Bottom board is square; measure, mark and saw it to the desired length. Check that one end of the board you will cut Sides and Ends from is square. Measure, mark and saw two pieces exactly as long as the Bottom is wide. These are the Ends. Cut each Side to equal length of Bottom plus two times the thickness of an End.

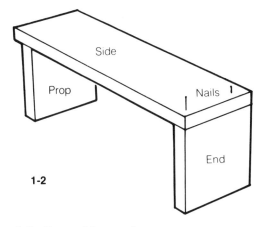

1-2

1-2. Reread the section on *Nails and Hammering* and the manufacturer's instructions for the glue you intend to use.

Glue and nail through Side into End. Make sure you have this butt joint held square and perpendicular when you nail it.

Remember: glue-nail joints are most easily done when you (1) start the nails first, (2) spread the glue, and (3) prop and hold securely while you finish nailing. Propping and holding are most easily accomplished by using the second End as shown, just set under the opposite end of the Side you are working on. In other words, you prop up the board you want to nail through so it is level. Obviously, you need a smooth level surface to work on.

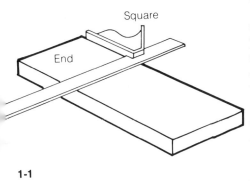

1-1

1-3. Glue and nail through Side into Bottom and through attached End into Bottom. Glue and nail opposite End on. Each time, turn the partially assembled piece so you are nailing a butt joint that is held square and perpendicular.

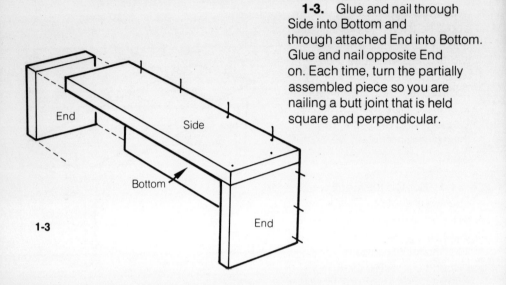

End

Side

Bottom

1-3

End

1-4. Turn box on Side already nailed and glued, then glue and nail remaining Side in place.

Side

1-4

1-5. Wipe up excess glue
and put box aside to let glue set.
Then sand smooth in
preparation for finishing.

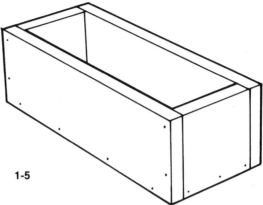

1-5

Project 2

TOOL TOTE

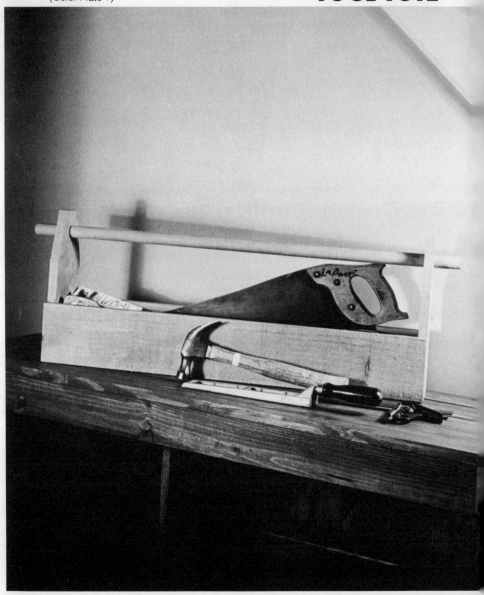

This is almost exactly the same as Project 1 except that the two Ends are made from the same thickness and width material as the Bottom; only the Sides might be of thinner stock. Consider the length of your hand saw and the weight of the wood you want to use to determine the size of of the Bottom. (A large tote can get quite heavy even before you load it up.) The dimensioned detail given at 2-1 is a suggestion only. The project will work with a board about 4" to 6" wide. We used a 1" dowel for the handle.

2-1. To make the Ends, first cut them to length. Mark the center line and measure down at least 1¾" to mark the center for the handle hole. Then make the angle cuts as indicated. It is hard to get a saw started at this low angle but a saber saw is easier to control provided you clamp on a guide strip first. Turn the board over to make the cut from the other edge.

To bore the hole with an auger bit, drill through until the screw point of the bit breaks the surface on the back side. Remove it and complete the hole by drilling from back to front. If you have no vise, clamp your work. Repeat for the opposite End so that both Ends are identical.

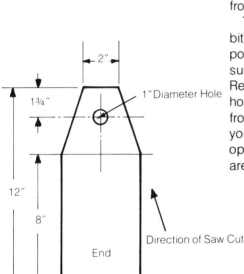

2-1

Note: If you do not have an auger bit, cut the dowel the same length as the Bottom. Drill and countersink the two End pieces so the Handle can be glued and screwed between the Ends rather than running through them as shown.

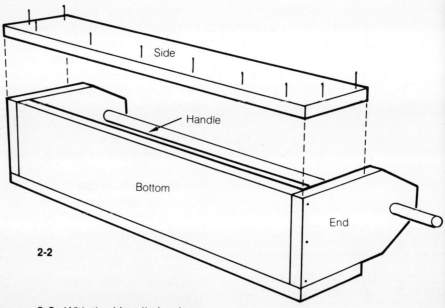

2-2

2-2. With the Handle in place, glue and nail both Ends to the Bottom. Then glue and nail on each Side.

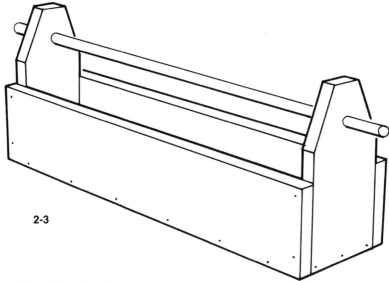

2-3

2-3. If the Handle slips
around in the hole, a nail into it
just inside the End will keep it
from pulling all the way out. Use
a nail against each End if it is
really loose. Prepare the Tote for
finishing if any is desired.
Otherwise just check for
splintery edges and take off the
sharpest corners.

Project 3

CUBE LAMP

To make the closed cube base, you will need six pieces of wood, all alike and all cut to the same length. That length is equal to the width of the board you use plus two times its thickness. The wood we used was from a nicely weathered pallet and measured 4¹³/₁₆" wide by a full ½" thick. What you find to use will greatly affect the shade and lamp parts selection you will make. We'll deal with generalities in that area though you'll have to get into specifics. For the wiring parts of this project you will need a knife or blade of some sort for stripping insulation from lamp cord, a small wrench for the locknuts and a small screwdriver for making the socket connections. But first the closed cube base.

3-1. With six pieces, identical and cut the same length, select one for the Top. Draw diagonal lines on the underside of it as indicated. At the intersection is the center of the piece. Drill a ⁷/₁₆" hole. If you're using an auger bit, you know how (see page 69). If you're using a twist drill bit or a power drill, always back up your work. That is, put a piece of scrap wood under it where you expect the point of the drill to come through. Clamp Top and scrap to something stationary. Drill straight (perpendicular). You'll know by feel and a change in the color of the sawdust when you are through the Top.

Mark with perpendicular lines and drill a hole in the piece you've selected for the Back. The wire will come out here so you want it to be above the Bottom piece of your cube. Make dimension "X" equal to the thickness of the Bottom plus ⅜" and drill a ¼" hole, backing your work as before.

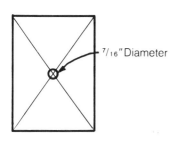

⁷/₁₆" Diameter

Top

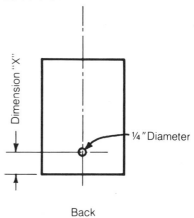

Dimension "X"

¼" Diameter

Back

3-1

3-2. The problem here is one of locating the Top on the edge of the Side. One easy way to do it is make a dry run. Set the two Side pieces up on edge as shown. Lay the Top piece across and simply hold the Front and Back pieces in place while you align the works and mark where the Top should come on the Side edge. Then, using the other Side as a prop, glue and nail the Top to the Side as shown.

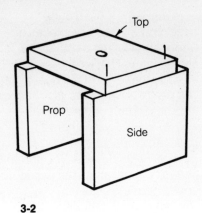

3-2

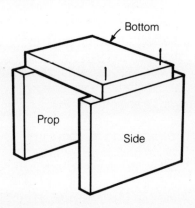

3-3

3-3. Repeat 3-2 for the Bottom and second Side, using the handiest loose pieces as your gauge, then prop as before and glue and nail through Bottom into Side.

3-4. Looks a bit like a porcupine, doesn't it? The point is you need now to glue and nail all but the Back together. It is easiest to glue and nail through Front into Top and Bottom first, using Back as prop. Then rotate cube to get other nails in. You will be handling a glued but not nailed assembly while you do this so watch out for dribbles. Nail through each Side into the Front and through the Bottom into the first Side.

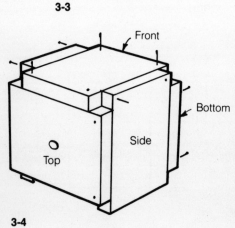

3-4

3-5. Nail through Top into second Side. That should complete 5 sides of your cube, leaving only the Back free. Wipe up excess glue. (Check the Back, just in case.) Now you are ready for the wiring. The start will be the same for just about anything. A short nipple or threaded lamp pipe goes through the hole in the top. It is held by a locknut above the Top and a washer and a locknut below, a general but pretty safe assumption (see 3-5 drawing).

Run the wire through the hole in the Back with the plug end *outside* the Back, naturally, and up through the nipple. Tape or otherwise hold the Back in place temporarily and go see your lampshade source. Find a retailer in your area who stocks lamp parts. If you have no parts on hand, go shopping with the bare base.

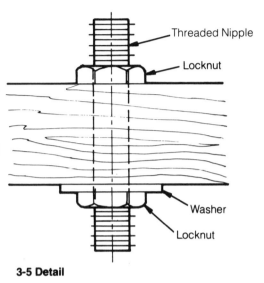

3-5 Detail

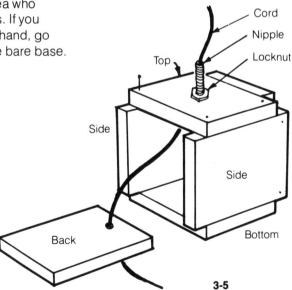

3-5

3-6. A wire with the plug already on it comes in the Lamparts Make-a-Lamp Kit, along with two nipples, locknut, threaded neck, socket and a 10″ harp with finial. We added a check ring and a threaded spindle to use the folded paper lampshade we selected. Size is all-important in making these choices. The actual wiring consists of pushing the wire up through to the socket which is screwed to the top of the nipple. Take the socket apart; cut, strip and twist each of the two stranded wires encased in the lamp cord and attach one under each screw terminal of the socket base. Put the works back together and tighten it all up. It's a good idea to tie an overhand knot in the cord inside the Back but do it loosely (before you push the end up through), then work the knot to the right position to pull up against the inside of the Back after you've glued and nailed that on to finish the lamp base. Set harp into harp wing. Set shade in place and tighten down the finial to hold it there. Put a bulb in and switch it on.

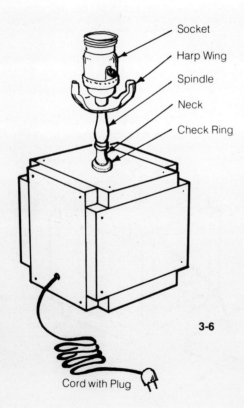

Socket

Harp Wing

Spindle

Neck

Check Ring

3-6

Cord with Plug

Project 4

DOG BED

4-1. First, measure the dog. Get him to lie down on his side comfortably extended. Conveniently, if he'll cooperate, on a piece of paper you can mark on. The object is to determine a rectangle sized to fit him. It ought to be 3″ to 6″ or 8″ bigger than he is on all four sides (3″ for a really small dog; be more generous with larger ones). You will need two pieces of fabric this size to make the pillow. We used denim backed with iron-on fusible interfacing to give it more body. With a ¾″ seam allowance, right sides together, stitch all around except for 6″ to 8″ left open to stuff. We used two pounds of polyester fiber in a pillow about 22″ x 27″. Use more if you want it fatter and firmer or use shredded foam or other stuffing if that is to your liking. Sew up the fill hole. Check with the dog.

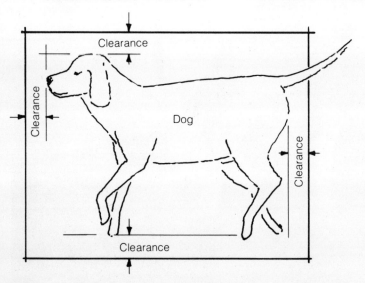

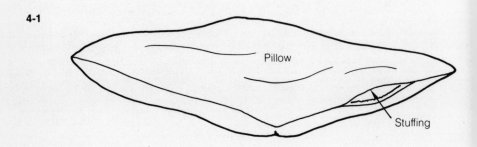

4-1

4-2. Using some of the smaller sticks you've secured (on the order of 1″ x 1″), make a frame-on-edge slightly smaller than the finished pillow measures.

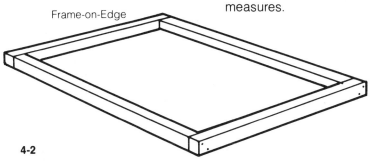

Frame-on-Edge

4-2

4-3. Using whatever you have enough of that will take the weight of the dog, glue and nail strips across for the dog bed Bottom assembly. You can also use plywood if you've found a piece large enough. If you space the strips, keep the spaces narrower than the dog's feet are. This makes a "slatted-frame-on-edge."

Make sure all the slats are flush with the frame-on-edge. Cut two Ends the same length as the Bottom assembly is wide. You'll select the width of these to suit the dog and what you have available. Cut a Back and a Front from the same material the length of the slatted frame-on-edge plus two times the thickness of the End material.

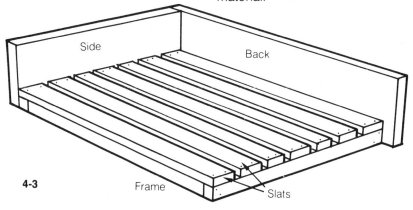

Side

Back

4-3   Frame   Slats

4-4. Cut out a section of the Front as indicated. Make it even with the top of the Pillow when that is in place. The curves are no problem with a saber saw. If you don't have one, make the Front of a narrower board and skip cutting out anything.

Shape the edges, rounding them all off carefully. If you used a narrow board Front, put a good radius on the front corners of the Ends. (Round them off well.) Glue and nail Front, Ends and Back in position, wiping off excess glue right away. This makes another frame-on-edge around the slatted frame. Glue and nail through Front and Back into Ends, too. When glue is dry, round all top edges, sand smooth and apply finish. When that is done and really dry, put the pillow in place and explain to the dog it's his new bed.

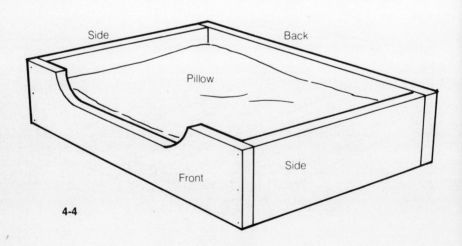

4-4

TABLE LAMP

For a lamp to go on a lamp table that is 24" or 25" high the light socket wants to be 16" to 18" above the table top if it is to work as a reading light. Ours is sized more generously with a base 19" high, the socket 22" from the table top and a 19" drum shade, 17" in diameter at the bottom.

A decorative accessory such as a lamp is certainly one place to use something that strikes you as being attractive. We found narrow slats on weathered pallets, hardwood but worth the effort, that could be used. You may find enough wider boards or you may find narrower strips more to your liking. You might even find enough moulding scraps to build into an interesting lamp base. Almost anything will work with the general approach outlined here. Enough pieces 18" or 19" long to build a rectangle 5" x 5" or 5" x 6" or even larger with a still larger bottom extension of some sort will do it. We will suggest how to duplicate the lamp shown and invite you to vary the design to use the materials you've scrounged.

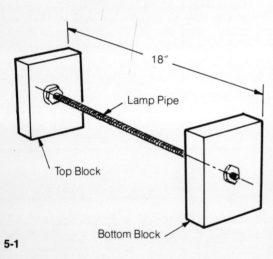

18"

Lamp Pipe

Top Block

Bottom Block

5-1

5-1. Using 2½" wide strips of ½" thick weathered wood, eight pieces were cut to 19" length. Two blocks of 2x6 rafter scraps were cut and ripped to fit inside as shown. (Note that the purpose served is that of battening the two-boards-per-side rectangle as well as providing a place to anchor the lamp works to. You could use plywood or separate strips to do the same thing.) We used 1/8 IP all-thread lamp pipe, cutting it to 20" from a 30" piece. (Should you have occasion to cut threaded pipe, use a hacksaw. Spin two locknuts onto the pipe across the spot you have marked off for the cut. Make the cut with the hacksaw. "Back out" the locknuts gently over the cut threads. File lightly to get rid of any light burrs if you have to, but don't file too much. You'll ruin the threads. Save the cut-off piece too. You may want to make a 10" lamp someday.) Using the threaded pipe and some locknuts, we mounted the Top and Bottom blocks 18" apart.

5-2. We glued and nailed on the Front and Back Strips plus one set of Side Strips to the blocks, keeping the strips flush at the Top block which makes the Bottom block inset 1". A "V" notch was made in the Back for the lamp cord. Make whatever adjustments are required to have the wire come out the bottom of the Back properly and use an insulated staple to hold the lamp cord to the Bottom block. We added a piece of wood to finish off the top of the lamp base, removing, then replacing, the top locknut. The External Battens to fit around the base were cut at this time, too, from strips of the weathered hardwood 1½" wide and ½" thick. The Back Batten was notched to match the V cut in the Back.

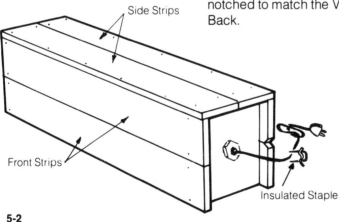

Side Strips

Front Strips

Insulated Staple

5-2

5-3. Proceed with the wiring as you did for the Cube Lamp, page 75, leaving the second Side and its Batten loose until you are satisfied with the wiring. Then close up the lamp base by gluing and nailing the remaining pieces in place. To accommodate the shade we selected, we used a 12" harp and added a knurled nut between spindle and neck. Otherwise the parts are the same as for the Cube Lamp.

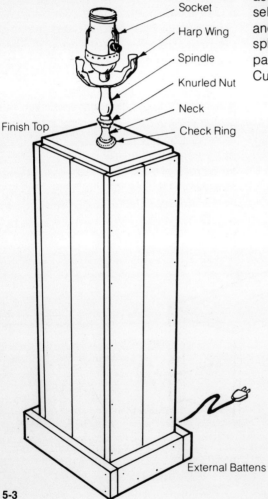

Socket

Harp Wing

Spindle

Knurled Nut

Neck

Finish Top

Check Ring

External Battens

5-3

Project 6

(Color Plate 1) **MIRROR**

Secure the unframed mirror first as all dimensions depend on what size it is. There's no right or wrong size, just something big enough to see into that will look well-proportioned in the most attractive boards you've scrounged. If your mirror is over a foot square, you'll need something ⅜" or more thick and upwards of 3" wide for the Face Frame. But remember you have to hang the thing up, so don't get it too heavy.

For the Back Frame, you'll need strips thicker than the mirror and wide enough to glue and nail in place securely. To back up the mirror, use one, two, or more pieces of corrugated cardboard a bit larger than the mirror, plus a piece of plywood or hardboard the same size. You will need to measure and figure fairly accurately on this project.

6-1. First, measure the mirror. Cut two pieces for the Face Frame Sides ½" *shorter* than the height of the mirror. Cut two pieces (Face Frame Top and Face Frame Bottom) from the same material. Make these equal in length to the width of the mirror plus two times the width of the Face Frame material *minus ½"*.

Lay out these four pieces face down on a flat surface. Check for squareness. It is the center opening that matters. It should overlap the mirror size ¼" on each edge. Get the mirror out of the way. Protect your work surface and working carefully to set the pieces properly without smearing, glue the meeting edges and hold with corrugated or other patented fasteners.

Add ⅛" to the width dimension of the mirror. Cut Back Frame Top and Bottom

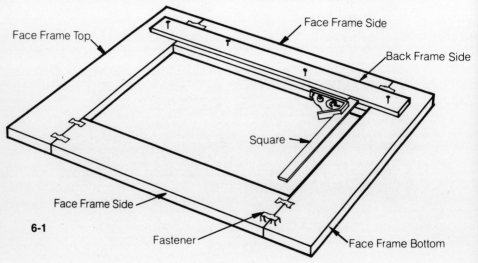

6-1

pieces to this dimension. Add ⅛" to the height dimension of the mirror plus the width of the Back Frame Top and Back Frame Bottom. Cut the Back Frame Side pieces to that dimension. Set your combination square to project ⁵/₁₆" so that when you use it as shown you can locate the Back Frame Sides properly.

Using the square, *tack* the Back Frame Sides in place as shown. Tack here means to nail fast but do not drive the nails all the way in. You are going to pull them out in a minute.

6-2. With the Back Frame Sides tacked in position, glue and nail the Back Frame Top and Bottom in place using the square to get the set-back right. Now remove the Back Frame Sides, apply the glue and nail them in place. Measure the opening (check that it is still square, too) and cut your cardboard and plywood (or hardboard) to fit snugly within it. You want a stack of backers which, plus the mirror thickness, will be the same as the thickness of the Back Frame material.

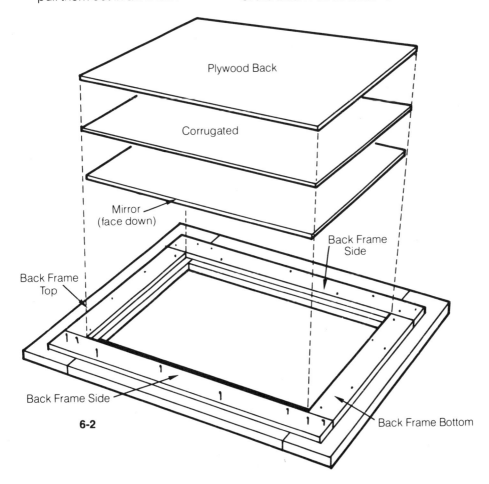

6-2

6-3. Set the mirror in place backed by the cardboard and plywood so the surface of the plywood and the surface of the Back Frame members are flush. Use strips of plywood or hardboard as shown to keep the mirror in place, or use narrower strips on all four edges overlapping the backer board, or cut a neatly removed large tin can end in quarters and use one piece in each corner to accomplish the same end.

Set your square so the blade projects one-quarter or one-fifth of the total height dimension. Use that to gauge the position of the screweyes. Reset the square to gauge the distance in from the side edges for centering the screweyes. Insert hanging wire through both screweyes, twist the ends together, then wrap the twisted part around the cross wire to secure it. Cut off wire.

If the Face Frame was made of attractive wood, you'll want to leave it alone. Otherwise, see the section on finishing.

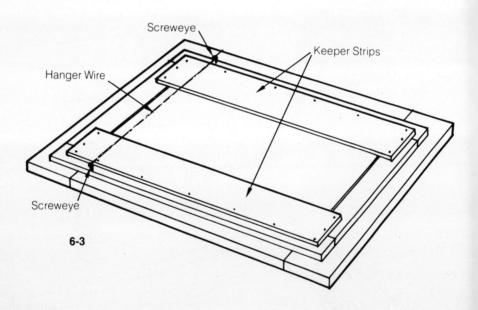

6-3

Project 7

TEA-FOR-TWO TABLE

89

Tables come in all sorts of sizes and styles. The ones in this series obviously will take advantage of the Open Frame concept teamed with the frame-on-edge idea to form an open cube. Planked battens form the tops and, depending on what the use is to be, a shelf or a cross brace is added to increase the stability. Construction order is essentially identical for all three tables.

Figuring out dimensions is the first step. For a table to eat at, a table top height of about 29" to 30" is usual. For space for the dishes, an accepted figure is 12" to 15" deep by 22" or more in width for each person. Foot room takes a good 22" too, especially if you may be trying to avoid a not-too-smooth edge. (You'll learn to round edges and sand well when you get to using some of the furniture you build.)

Sizing the top will depend somewhat on the width of the boards you have available, too. You don't want to have to rip-saw if you can possibly avoid it. So figure 22" plus four times the thickness of the wood you'll be using for the Open Frames as the absolute minimum dimension in that direction. If you have enough boards the same thickness and at least 30" long to work out to at least 2" over your minimum dimension, cut the two aprons to the minimum dimension and be satisfied with a 2" overhang though 3" or 4" on each side would look better. Cut the length of the Planked Top to give the same overhang, that is, to extend beyond the Apron the same amount that the Top extends beyond the Open Frames. That dimension, less the overhangs allowed, less the thickness of the two Aprons, will be the length of the Outer Frame Top and Bottom. The Outer Frame sides will equal 30" less the thickness of the table top and total width of Outer Frame Top and Bottom. That establishes the size of your Open Frame. The Inner Frame Side will of course be equal to the 30" less table top thickness (the same as the total of Outer Frame Side length plus width of Outer Frame Top and Bottom). The Inner Frame Top equals the length of the Outer Frame Top less the width of the two Inner Frame Sides. The two Blocks plus the thickness of the Cross Brace will total this same dimension.

7-1. To assemble the Open Frames, lay out the parts dry as shown first, just to check your arithmetic. When you're sure it's right, glue and nail the two Frames, setting aside two of the Blocks for the present.

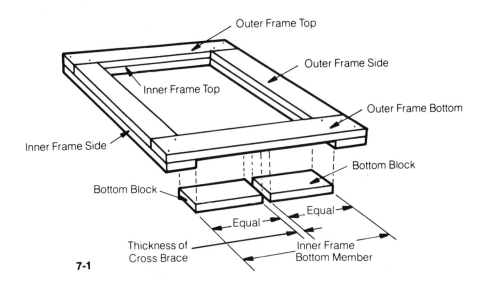

7-1

7-2. With the two Open Frames (Blocked Inner Frames as shown) held up on edge and parallel, glue and nail one Apron in place and check that all is square and parallel. Then glue and nail the Cross Brace in place. Move the assembly as little as possible to glue and nail the other Apron and the other two Blocks in place.

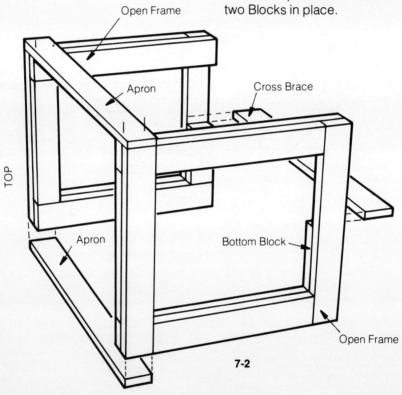

Open Frame

Apron

Cross Brace

TOP

Apron

Bottom Block

Open Frame

7-2

7-3. Set the assembled table
base up properly and again
check for squareness. Measure
the open area between Aprons
and Open Frames to determine
length and placement of the
wider Battens.

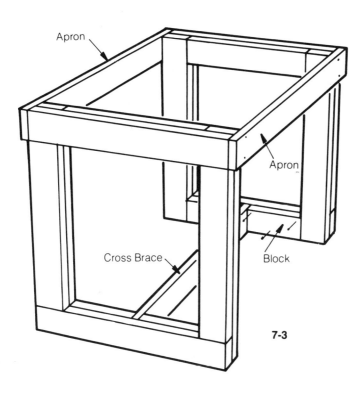

7-3

7-4. Cut Battens to length determined and center them in width of the underside of the table top. If you want to, clamp a strip about where the optional edge Batten is indicated on top of the loose planks so they will stay put while you glue and nail on the wider Battens. Once they have set, you can glue and nail on the optional Battens, keeping them clear of the Apron. If you have an overhang of more than 3″, you have room enough for the additional battens which will help keep the table top flat.

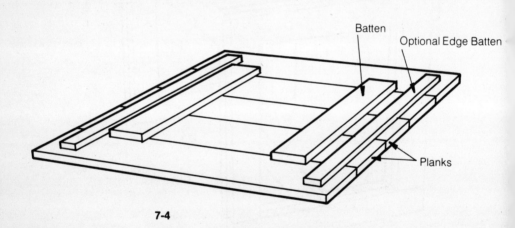

Batten

Optional Edge Batten

Planks

7-4

7-5. We found the planked tops heavy enough to stay put without gluing and nailing them to the table bases on this table and the coffee table, but if you want to pick up the table by the top and get the whole table, glue and nail the top on.

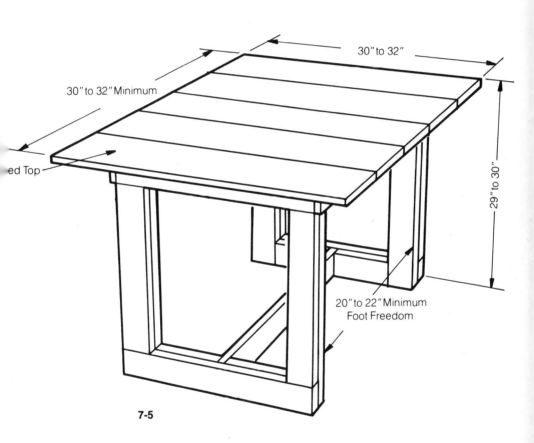

30" to 32"

30" to 32" Minimum

29" to 30"

ed Top

20" to 22" Minimum
Foot Freedom

7-5

Note: Keep on figuring and you'll see how easily the line of reasoning that resulted in your Tea-for-Two table can be developed into this Two-plus-Two Table. The simplest way (though not necessarily the best way) is, in effect, to add on a second table. Let the apron pieces run the full length of both units. One set of Outer Frame Top, Sides and Bottom parts, serving as the center layer of the middle support shown, is common to both units. Add a few more Top Planks and you AND your guests will have space to dine.

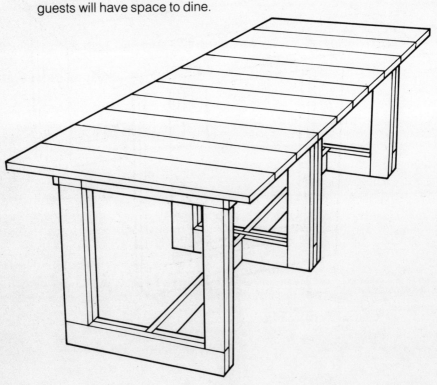

Color Plate 1

1. Hanging Lantern, page 136.   2. Mirror, page 85.   3. Table Lamp, page 81.   4. Cube Lamp, page 72. 5. Tool Tote, page 68.   6. Dog Bed, page 77.   7. Plant Box, page 64.

Color Plate 2

Tea-for-Two Table, page 89. Chairs, page 142. Four-Foot Modular Unit (*top*), page 131. Doored Modular Unit (*bottom left*), page 121. Drawered Modular Unit (*bottom right*), page 126.

Color Plate 3

Child's Chair, page 149. Toy Chest, page 112. Four-Foot Modular
Unit, page 131.

Color Plate 4

Open Shelf Modular Unit (*top*), page 117. Doored Modular Unit (*bottom left*), page 121. Four-Foot Modular Unit (*right*), page 131.

Color Plate 5

Coffee Table, page 109. Loveseat, page 157. Armchair, page 152.
Footstool, page 160. Lamp Table, page 105. Table Lamp, page 81.

Color Plate 6

Desk, page 165. Cube Lamp, page 72. Open Shelf Modular Unit (*top*), page 117. Four-Foot Modular Unit (*bottom*), page 131.

Color Plate 7

Bed, page 168.

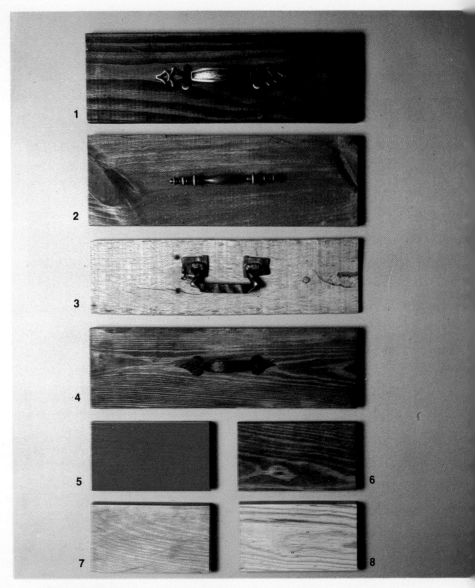

Color Plate 8

1. Dark walnut stain; Mediterranean hardware with antique brass finish.   2. Mahogany stain; traditional hardware with antique copper finish.   3. Weathered hardwood with no finish; frontier colonial hardware with antique silver finish.   4. Walnut stain; Early American hardware with wrought iron finish.   5. One coat of enamel paint on pine.   6. Walnut stain on pine.   7. Grey stain on pine.   8. Clear varnish on pine.   Pages 176–179.

(Color Plate 5)   # LAMP TABLE

Just to keep you on your toes, we've reversed the Inner Frame and Outer Frame direction on the Lamp Table from what it was on the Tea Table. Also, you'll see by comparing the two that the Planked Top runs parallel to the Apron rather than across it. By the time you figure out the dimensions for cutting the parts, you'll tumble to the adaptability of the Open Frames as table legs.

A lamp table is usually about 20" to 22" high and often 24" square, though it can be larger and doesn't have to be square. An attractive size is 14" by 28". See what you have available in planks (all the same thickness) for the Top that will work out with two or three similar (though not necessarily as thick) planks for the Shelf below.

8-1. Once you have the Open Frames to the dry run stage, assembly is essentially the same as before, except there need not be an Outer Frame Top and we use a shelf rather than a cross brace to hold the bottom of the Open Frames parallel. So glue and nail the Open Frames as shown.

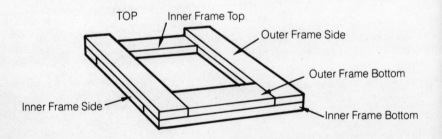

8-1

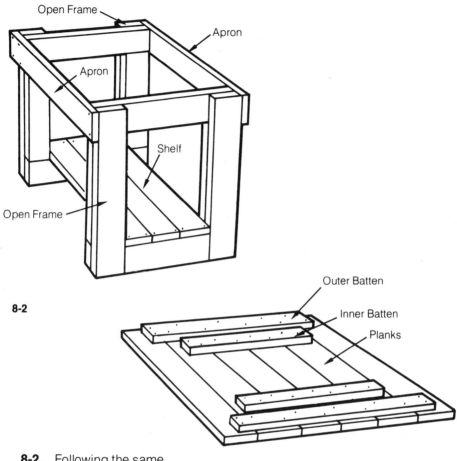

Open Frame

Apron

Apron

Shelf

Open Frame

8-2

Outer Batten

Inner Batten

Planks

8-3

8-2. Following the same order as before, glue and nail Apron, Shelf and the second Apron in place, forming the bottom of the Lamp Table.

8-3. Measure the open area and mark the planked top for locating the Inner Battens. Use the Outer (Optional) Batten or not, as you think advisable. Glue and nail Battens in place.

8-4.   Glue and nail Planked
Top to completed base. Now
you have something to put
Project 5 on top of.

Planked Top

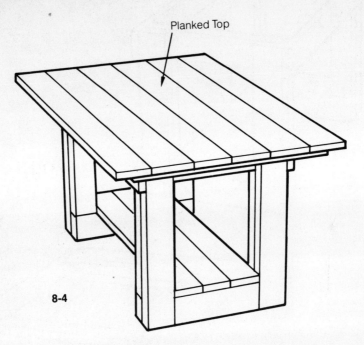

8-4

Project 9

COFFEE TABLE

Now that you've cut up all the long boards to make small table tops we'll tell you what to do to make long boards out of short ones. The Coffee Table is made just like the Lamp Table except there is an Outer Frame Top shown. Coffee tables can be any size actually, though they are often around 4' long by 16" wide and generally about 15" or 16" high. Many times they are used in front of a sofa, hence the abundance of the long rectangular shapes.

9-1. Taking stock of what you have on hand, you'll figure cutting lengths as before for the Open Frames. Note: if you are using boards under ½" in actual thickness for the shelf and you've made it over 5' long, consider the advisability of adding a third Open Frame at the midpoint. If that is where you file your magazines, do it. Dry run and then glue and nail up the Open Frames.

9-2. Just as you did before, assemble the Table Bottom and measure the opening.

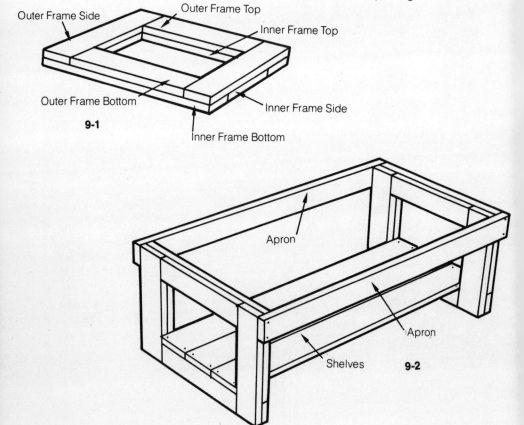

Outer Frame Side

Outer Frame Top

Inner Frame Top

Outer Frame Bottom

Inner Frame Side

9-1

Inner Frame Bottom

Apron

Apron

Shelves

9-2

9-3. Arrange what boards you have for the Top and selecting more of the same thickness see if you can't work out end-to-end joins (not in the outer planks) at attractive locations that can be supported by additional battens as shown.

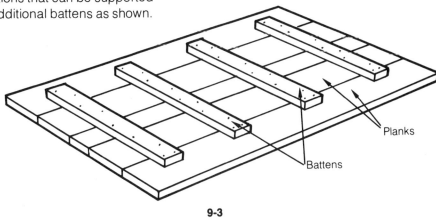

Planks

Battens

9-3

9-4. Glue and nail on the top, unless you move a lot, since it is easier to transport two pieces than one.

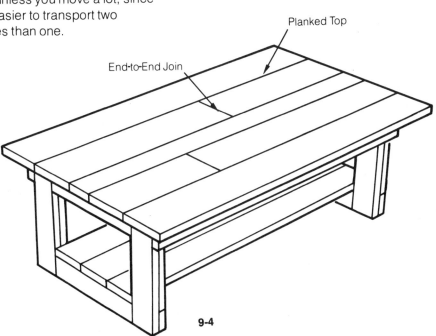

Planked Top

End-to-End Join

9-4

(Color Plate 3)

TOY CHEST

Shown as a Toy Chest, this same approach would make you a hope chest or blanket chest or any other kind of chest you cared to call it, depending on what size you chose to make it. For toys, 1′ high by 1′ wide by 2′ long seemed like minimum good dimensions. See how wide the boards you have are and make the top a little larger on the Ends and Front Edges. With an overhang, you don't need a pull

to lift the lid and it is a lot more comfortable not sitting on one.

The Planked Frame concept is introduced carefully here because when you get to building the next few projects you will really want to know how to get things square. If you have a work place with an expendable top, nail on the Jig Strip; otherwise, use clamps. Either way, make sure you select a straight piece to align to.

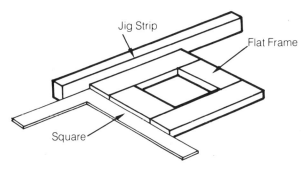

10-1

10-1. With the size of the Ends established, square up a Flat Frame as shown. Cut Planks to this length.

10-2. Glue and nail Planks to Flat Frame. Make two Ends exactly alike.

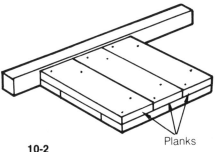

10-2

10-3. With the top edges of the Planked Frames down, glue and nail the Bottom Planks in place, making sure you have the Ends parallel. Turn the assembly so you can nail and glue Front and Back Planks on evenly too. You may want to use scrap strips tacked temporarily to front and back edges of the Frames to keep things square as you establish the joint.

10-4. Measure inside the completed box and set the Battens in place so they will clear as you open the Lid. Remember the back edge (hinged edge) of the Lid and the Back of the box will be flush, the overhang all at the front edge. Glue and nail up the Lid.

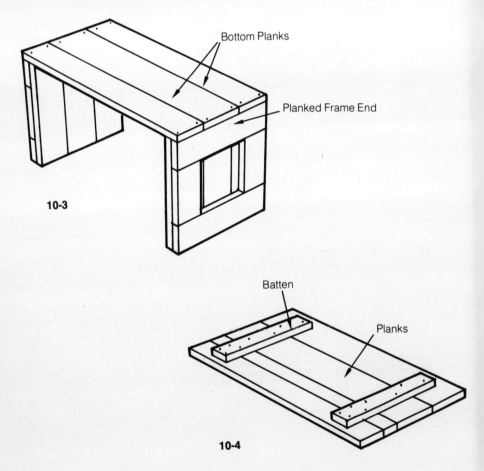

Bottom Planks

Planked Frame End

10-3

Batten

Planks

10-4

10-5.   You can use a piano hinge if you like, though a pair of butt hinges will be a lot less expensive. Align hinge pin with the line where Lid and box meet and try it gently before you drive the screws in tight. We installed two hinge straps on the Chest, too.

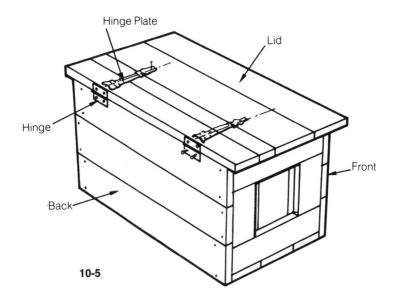

10-5

MODULAR UNITS

One of the most intelligent ways to provide storage units is to settle on a method and build everything the same way, sticking shelves in and doors on or converting to drawers within the same shell design. If the shells are made in identical sizes or in multiples of a base size, they can be stacked, rearranged and recombined again and again. We settled on a base module 36" high, 16" deep and 24" wide and built one double length unit (Project 14) 48" long, 24" high and 16" deep. All *Modular Units* consist basically of two Planked Frame ends held parallel and perpendicular by three or four External Battens, which incidentally form a frame-on-edge in the horizontal plane around the top and bottom of each unit. The tops are all planked. A wider unit requires a simple center divider of Battened Planks to carry out the concept easily.

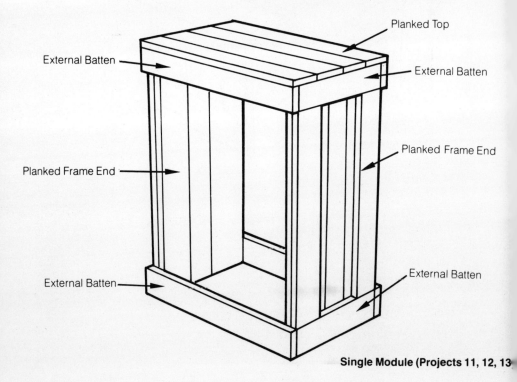

Planked Top

External Batten

External Batten

Planked Frame End

Planked Frame End

External Batten

External Batten

Single Module (Projects 11, 12, 13)

OPEN SHELF
MODULAR UNIT

(Color Plates 4 and 6)

First, check your wood pile. A 16" depth is not sacred. You will need a good supply of boards whose total width will make up to a dimension around 16", and you will need a lot of boards for Tops too. It will probably be smart to select stock dimension lumber for the Tops so that when you build more next year it will still be possible to duplicate the planking size. A little fudging in spacing the vertical planks behind the Flat Frame of the ends can accommodate slight irregularities in width, too.

11-1. To build any modular unit, start by making up the Planked Ends to the exact size you have established: that is, whatever will add up to around 16" by 36" minus the thickness of what you will use for Top Planks. Lay the two Ends with their front edges together, insides up facing you. Locate one Cleat at the bottom to align with the External Battens to come. Locate the second Cleats where you want the mid-shelf. Glue and nail in place. These cleats will be the full width of the Planked End. Double check that all are square.

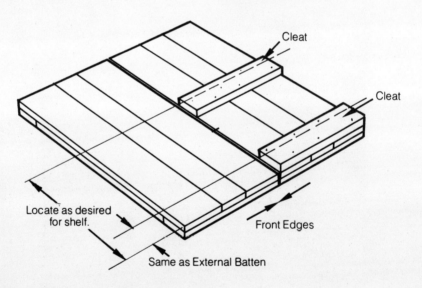

Cleat

Cleat

Locate as desired for shelf.

Front Edges

Same as External Batten

11-1

11-2. Set the two planked Ends up on their front edges and glue and nail on the three External Battens across the back, aligning them with the Cleats inside and with the top edge.

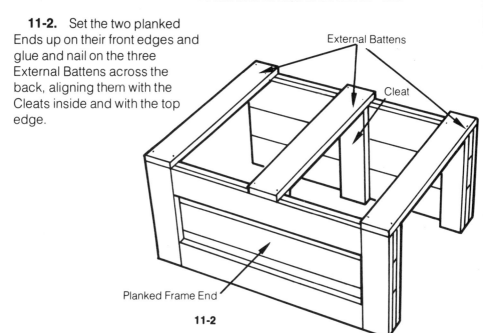

External Battens

Cleat

Planked Frame End

11-2

11-3. Glue and nail on the External Batten across the bottom front. Cut the boards for the two shelves to fit between the Planked Frame Ends and select them to come out flush with the External Battens front and back, as shown. Glue and nail in the Bottom Shelf as shown, then the center front Batten and that Shelf, then the top front Batten.

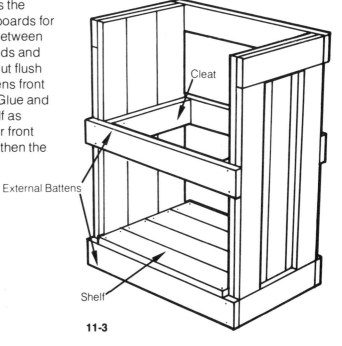

Cleat

Cleat

External Battens

Shelf

11-3

11-4.   Set the unit up and glue and nail on the Top Planks, making them flush with the External Battens. You can see how External Batten and horizontal members of the Planked Frames make a frame-on-edge in the horizontal plane at the top, at the bottom and, in this unit, at the middle.

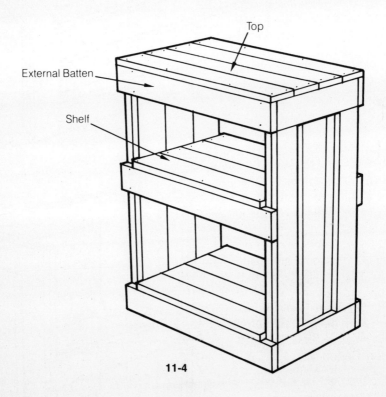

11-4

DOORED
MODULAR UNIT

(Color Plates 2 and 4)

12-1. Start this unit exactly the same way by making up the Planked Ends and laying them out square, front edges meeting, inside face up. Locate the Cleats as indicated. The Bottom Cleat plus the shelf thickness should total a bit more than the width of the External Batten as shown, so that here the Shelf will fit behind the Batten rather than on top of it. The mid-shelf or shelves can be located anywhere, as you desire. But align the back end of all Cleats in from the back edges of the Planked Ends the thickness of the Battened Plank Back.

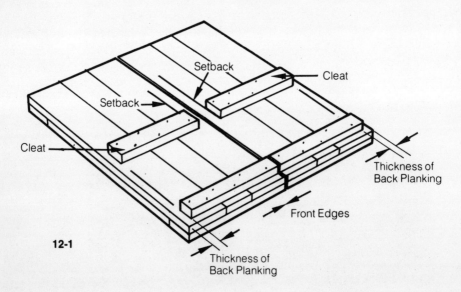

12-1

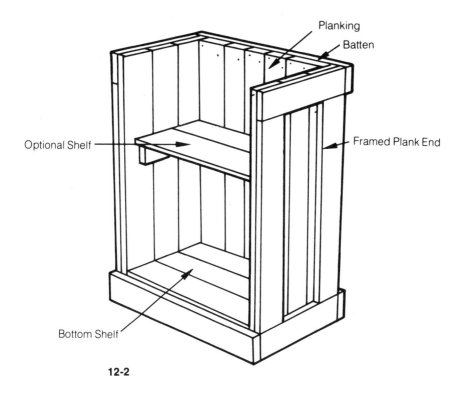

12-2

12-2. As before, with the Planked Ends on their front edges, glue and nail on the External Battens across the back and the bottom front. Now lay the shell on its back and fit the plank Back in. These planks will all be cut the same length as the Planked Frame Ends are, but this is the place to juggle the odd-width boards to make up the right width for the back dimension. Glue and nail them in place. Glue and nail in the bottom Shelf and then the optional mid-shelf. Set the unit upright, and glue and nail on the Top and the top front External Batten.

12-3. Make up a battened door as shown to fit between the front External Battens with good clearance and to align with the frame-to-plank joint of the ends. This means the Door will be lapped over the Planking on the Ends but set in the width of the Flat Frame, taking a flush overlay cabinet hinge. We used self-closing hinges, installing them about 4″ in from top and bottom of the door. Hold the hinge leaf in place on the inside surface of the door and mark one hole. Drill a pilot hole and set that screw. Try the hinges and finish attaching that leaf.

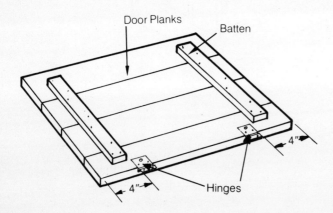

Door Planks

Batten

4″

4″

Hinges

12-3

12-4. You may as well drill and attach the pull, too, before attaching the door, following the manufacturer's directions. Lay the shell on its back and set the door in place with hinges on the edge of the Flat Frame. Mark, drill and run in screws lightly. Try the door. Finish driving the screws.

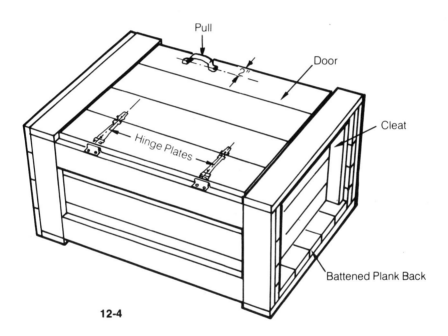

12-4

DRAWERED
MODULAR UNIT

(Color Plate 2)

One of the most difficult things to build is a good, square, nicely fitting, smoothly operating drawer, especially when you will do it with the rather limited tools we assume are all you have. The drawers shown are basic and as simple as we can devise. If you have a shaper or can run a dado on your table or radial arm saw, you probably already know how to make a lighter-weight, more accurate drawer and may well choose to do so.

The first problems you will have to solve are mathematical. You will, in a 36″ height, most likely want three drawers. What boards you have on hand will determine how you make up the False Drawer Fronts, teaming two or three together to make up the deeper drawers. You will need to juggle False Front dimension with Drawer Sides with location of Cleats to make the best use of what you have. Allow good clearance between False Fronts, and remember that each Cleat helps keep the drawer below in line, as well as giving the one above it something to ride on.

13-1. Construction of the unit still runs the same course. Planked Frame Ends are laid face down, front edges aligned. Locate, glue and nail the Cleats on as required, setting them in from the back edge to allow for the Battened Plank Back.

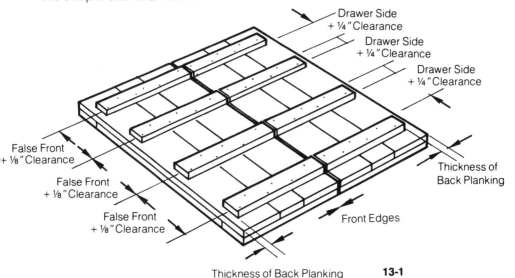

Drawer Side + ¼″ Clearance

Drawer Side + ¼″ Clearance

Drawer Side + ¼″ Clearance

False Front + ⅛″ Clearance

False Front + ⅛″ Clearance

False Front + ⅛″ Clearance

Thickness of Back Planking

Front Edges

Thickness of Back Planking **13-1**

13-2. With the unit on its front edges, glue and nail on the External Battens across the back and the bottom External Batten at the front. With the unit on its back, glue and nail in the Back Planking as before.

Planked Frame End   Battened Plank Back

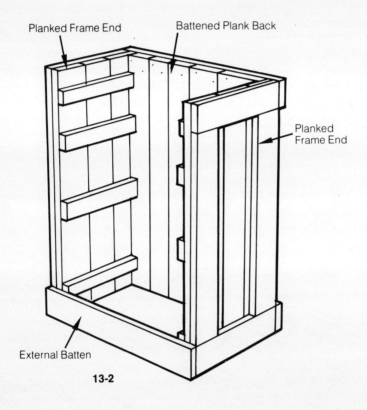

Planked Frame End

External Batten

13-2

13-3. To figure the size of the Drawer Front, take the inside dimension of the shell, subtract ⅛" clearance for each side and subtract the thickness of both Drawer Sides. The height of the Drawer Front should be such that the Bottom can be held on with a strip at least ⅜" thick and still take a Cleat at the Drawer Sides. You will probably find it easier to make Front, Sides and Back all flush at the top. The Bottom nails onto the Back which is glued and nailed between the Sides about ½" in from their ends. It is the Bottom of drawers that often give trouble with buckling, so if you're using a material that is apt to move with high humidity, seal the edges as soon as you have it cut to size. All the drawers are made the same way. Try sliding them on the Cleats now.

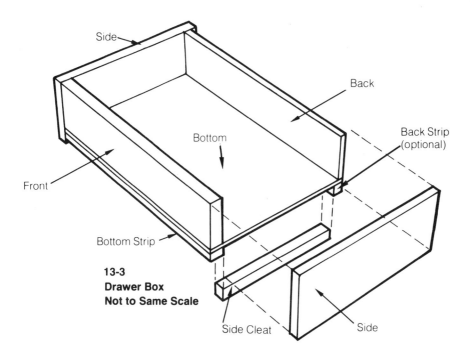

Side

Back

Back Strip
(optional)

Bottom

Front

Bottom Strip

13-3
Drawer Box
Not to Same Scale

Side Cleat

Side

13-4. With the drawer "boxes" set in place in the shell and the boards you will use for False Fronts cut to the length you've chosen (either align with the outside face of the Planked Frame Ends or with the frame-to-plank join, same as the Door was), tilt the unit back very slightly so you can lay the False Fronts in place, using match folders or other same-thickness shims to position them with proper clearance. When you are satisfied, tack through the False Front into the Drawer Front, as indicated. Then remove each drawer and glue and nail on the False Fronts more securely. Following the manufacturer's instructions, drill for the pulls. We used the bail pull style on these drawers. The screws that come with cabinet hardware usually assume a ¾" thickness for doors and drawers. You probably will have to buy longer machine screws to attach these pulls through two thicknesses of wood. Take one of the screws with you to make sure you get the proper size and threading. A little lubricant on the top of each Cleat will keep the drawers operating easily.

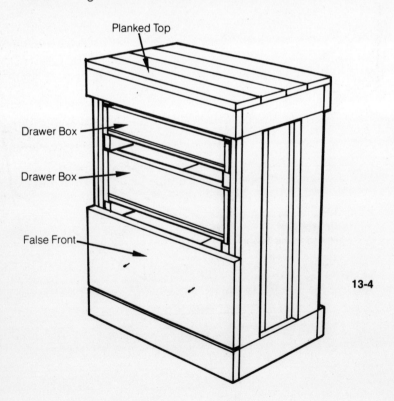

Planked Top

Drawer Box

Drawer Box

False Front

13-4

FOUR-FOOT MODULAR UNIT

131

14-1. As usual, start by making up the Planked Frame Ends. Next, construct a Planked Battened Center Divider to the same dimensions. This is most easily accomplished by propping up the planks, cut to the right length, on a couple of boards the same thickness as the Flat Frame part of the Ends. Join these planks with a Batten shorter by the thickness of the Planked Batten Back. If you'll figure the Front edges meeting as shown on the Center and the Left End, you'll have it right.

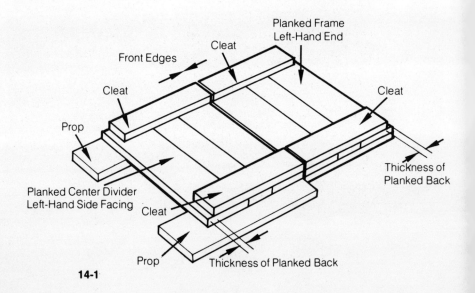

Planked Frame
Left-Hand End

Front Edges

Cleat

Cleat

Cleat

Prop

Thickness of
Planked Back

Planked Center Divider
Left-Hand Side Facing

Cleat

Prop

Thickness of Planked Back

14-1

14-2.   Turn the Center over to
the Right-Hand Side, facing up,
and butt the front edge of the
Right-Hand Planked Frame End
to it. Set the battens in from the
back edges a distance equal to
the thickness of the Planked
Batten Back. An optional shelf is
shown for which you'd need to
provide a Cleat set in from
the edges as indicated.

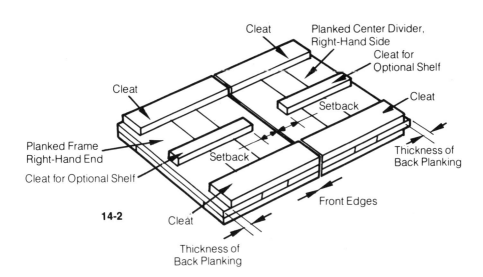

Cleat

Planked Center Divider,
Right-Hand Side

Cleat for
Optional Shelf

Cleat

Cleat

Setback

Cleat

Planked Frame
Right-Hand End

Setback

Thickness of
Back Planking

Cleat for Optional Shelf

Front Edges

14-2

Cleat

Thickness of
Back Planking

14-3.   Setting the two Ends and Divider up on their front edges, the two External Battens can be glued and nailed in place as before. Laying the unit on its back, the Planking for the Back is glued and nailed in place. Note that the Center Divider Planking glues directly to the two External Battens at the back. One can quit with this stage as soon as the Top Batten across the front is glued and nailed on and the Top planked if the unit is to go atop other units and consequently needs no toe mold.

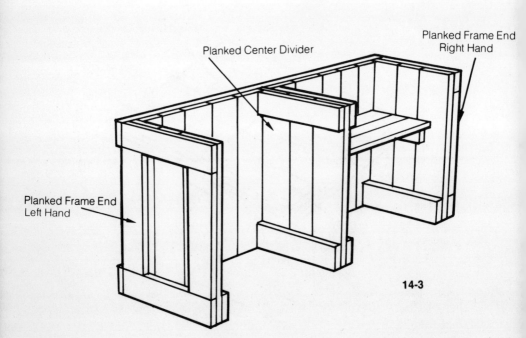

Planked Center Divider

Planked Frame End Right Hand

Planked Frame End Left Hand

14-3

14-4.   Otherwise, glue and nail the Bottom Front External Batten in place, glue and nail in the two Bottom Shelves, glue and nail in the optional shelf and glue and nail on the Top Batten and the Top Planking to finish the unit for use directly on the floor.

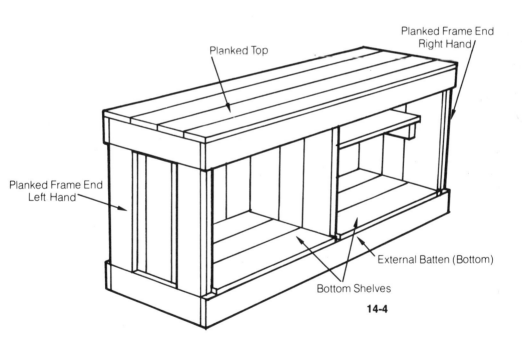

Planked Frame End Right Hand

Planked Top

Planked Frame End Left Hand

External Batten (Bottom)

Bottom Shelves

14-4

Project 15

HANGING LANTERN

136

It's time you had a little more variety so we've put this totally different project here. It will light up those practical, substantial pieces you've just completed and get you thinking about other materials as well as depleting your small-scrap woodpile.

In essence, this project is a cage for holding diffusing plastic around a light source. The plastic we used is White W-2447 Plexiglas®, ⅛" thick. Plexiglas softens with too much heat, so you must be sure to provide plenty of ventilation and not get the plastic too close to the light bulb. It should be allowed to move rather than buckle as it might if screwed into place. We worked with four pieces 7" wide by 12" high. You may have found scraps larger or smaller, or pieces of colored glass, or perhaps perforated hardboard or perforated metal that could be used in much the same way with the addition of thinner plastic. The magic is not in the exact diffusing material used so much as it is in covering the cage structure with scraps of wood cut to fit in an attractive arrangement that you work out from the scraps you have available. The wiring is made simple by using a hanging light kit and a porcelain socket adapter kit. Directions are provided on the packages. (You need to use a porcelain socket, because this is a base-up light that will get hot. Admit it and plan for it.)

15-1. The basic construction requires a Top and a Bottom notched at the corners to accept the four Corner Strips. The opening on each face of the Lantern should be ¼" less than the size of your plastic. That is, dimension W is 6¾" for our 7" wide plastic, and dimension H is 11¾" for our 12" height.

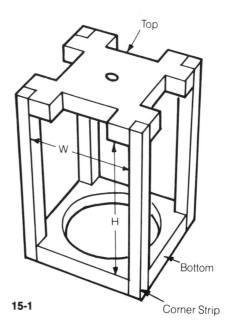

15-1

Top

W

H

Bottom

Corner Strip

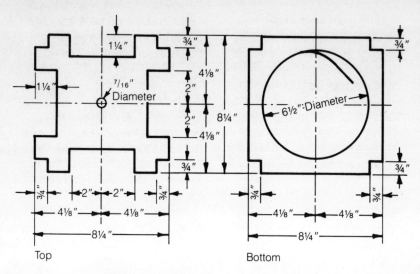

Top

Bottom

15-1
Details
Dimensions apply only if
you use 7" x 12" plastic, ⅛"
thick, and ¾" x ¾" actual
for Corner Strips.

15-1. Details. If you use that size Plexiglas, the dimensions worked out here will be right for you, with ¾" x ¾" Corner Strips 13¼" long if you use, as we did, ¾" plywood for Top and Bottom. Whatever size you go to, cut out the Top as much as possible (while still supporting the posts). Locating the center by the diagonal lines method, drill a ⁷⁄₁₆" hole there. On the Bottom, we made the circle cutout with a saber saw. It's called a "plunge cut" and may be a bit scary if you've never done it before. Tilt the saw up on the front edge of the shoe. Turn it on. Lower the blade into the wood firmly and determinedly until the whole shoe rests properly on the surface. Then cut on the line. You'll probably want to practice this once or twice. Don't try to hit the circle proper. Come inside and saw out to blend in to it, as indicated. You can also saw out an enclosed circle like this starting the blade in a hole bored big enough to fit it.

15-2. We used ⅛"thick hardboard cut into ⁹/₁₆"wide strips to frame the plastic on each side. The idea is to form a Flat Frame around the plastic with about ¹/₁₆"clear on all sides. Glue and nail the Strips to Top, Bottom and Corner Strips. We chose to mount the porcelain socket to the Top at this time too, following the directions illustrated on the back of the package.

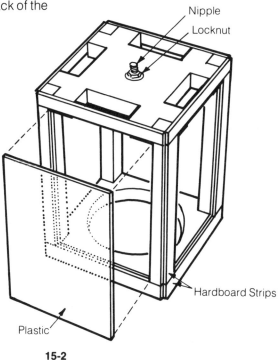

Nipple

Locknut

Hardboard Strips

Plastic

15-2

15-3. Now comes the creative part. Out of your stockpile of wood bits, strips and pieces, and working on one face at a time, select and sometimes cut pieces to overlap the join between plastic and Frame Strips, holding the plastic in place. Then find a few more blocks and strips to make a pleasing arrangement on each face of your lantern. We suggest a dry run first, then glue and nail each in place, keeping all glue off the plastic so it will continue to move freely. If you've used a perforated material for the diffuser panels, you won't want to get too involved in tiny blocks; settle for four plain strips on each face. If you've got a miter box you are dying to try out, you can make a picture frame for each face, stripping the joint at the corners with a simple quarter round. We happen to think the challenge of block fitting is more fun.

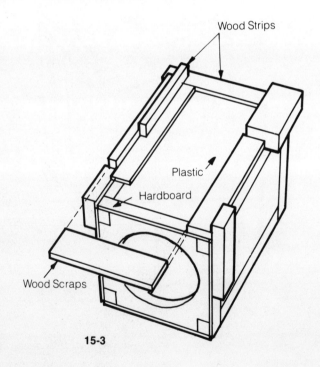

Wood Strips

Plastic

Hardboard

Wood Scraps

15-3

15-4. Wiring the works is simple. Just follow the manufacturer's directions and make sure the ceiling or wall on which you install the hanger hooks is strong enough to support the weight of your very own original-design lantern.

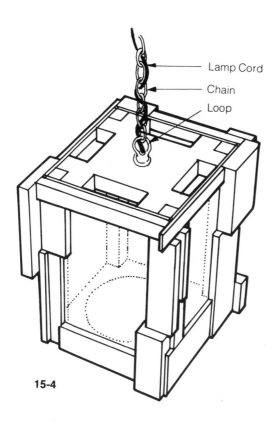

Lamp Cord

Chain

Loop

15-4

Project 16

CHAIR

142

Make a quick comparison of 16-2 with the bottom part of any of the three tables shown. You'll see right away that the chair design simply alters the Open-Frames-plus-Aprons concept a bit. The long Side Frame member is extended for the Outer Back Leg so that it supports the chair back and the Apron pieces set into instead of on the face of the two Open Frames to tie them together.

Anything built to sit on has to take into account the average size and proportion of the human bottom. Most dining and desk chairs have a full seat width of 16" to 17" and a full seat depth of at least 15". Seat height is usually about 17". The back should slope about 1" back from the seat depth line for every 5" up from the seat top. (What's between the back supports really doesn't count.) Watch where the dimensions are taken in these drawings. It's done to allow for the natural variations you'll have in the materials.

16-1. Start with a Frame-on-Edge for the Seat Frame. The overall dimensions will be the depth of seat plus the width of the Outer Back Leg material by the seat width less twice the thickness of the Outer Leg. Glue and nail the Seat Frame together.

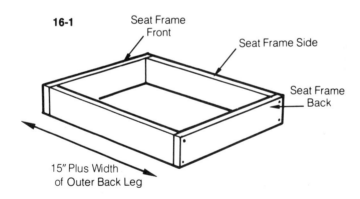

16-1 Seat Frame Front Seat Frame Side Seat Frame Back 15" Plus Width of Outer Back Leg

16-2. Cut the Inner Legs and Bottom Rail to complete the Inner Frame. Cut the Outer Legs and Outer Sides to lengths to fit as shown. Figure your Outer Back Leg taper and shape them too. Glue and nail together.

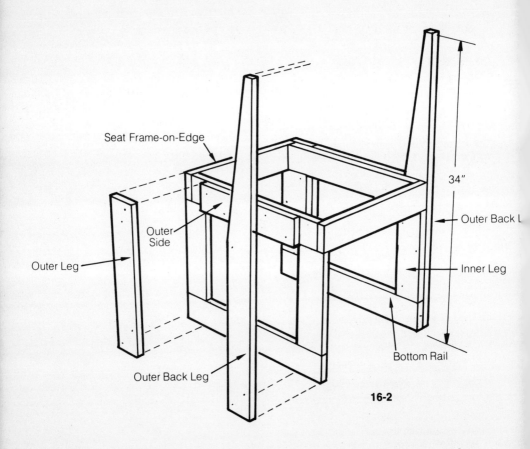

Seat Frame-on-Edge

Outer Side

Outer Leg

Outer Back Leg

34"

Outer Back L

Inner Leg

Bottom Rail

16-2

16-3 Detail

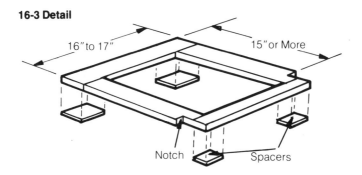

16" to 17"

15" or More

Notch

Spacers

16-3.   If you intend to
duplicate the macrame or rush
the seat, prepare the Flat Frame
as shown, gluing and fastening
the Frame together as a unit.
Notch the corners as indicated
to clear the Outer Back Legs.
(Beware: do not place a metal
fastener where you will cut it
making these notches.) Round
off all edges where the cord or
rush might rub and apply the
finish desired now, before
further assembly.

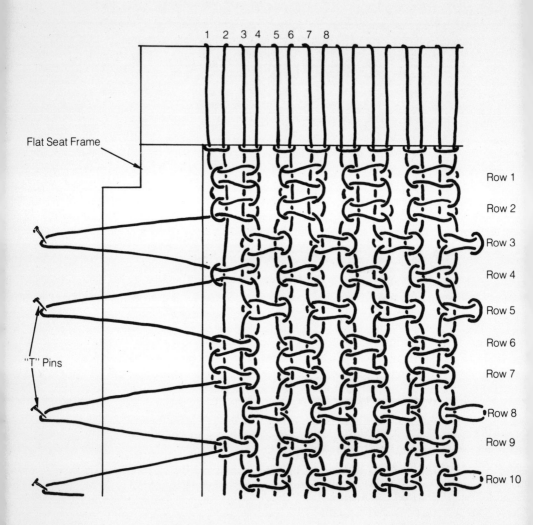

16-3 Detail

16-3. Detail. We used three balls (250 feet each) of #72 Cotton Seine Twine for the two chairs. Twelve groups of four working ends each will fit nicely on the Flat Frame we used. Check your Flat Frame opening and add or subtract in multiples of four. Figure working lengths at 4½ times the open area plus the front-to-back seat dimension plus about 16" for catching and tying under the seat proper.

If you want to dye the twine, use home-fabric dye, dissolving it in boiling water, then tempering it down a bit so you can stand to work in it. Skein the twine from the balls, tying the skeins loosely in three or four places and washing thoroughly to remove any sizing. Dye all three lengths simultaneously. Hot water makes the twine very kinky, so be prepared. Set your "C" clamps to measure off the lengths you require for one chair.

The macrame itself is extremely simple. Lark's head each doubled cut length around the Back Flat Frame Member, keeping ends even except on outside double. There set cord 1 about twice as long as cord 2 and lark's head in position. With each group of four working ends (1-2-3-4) make a sennit of two square knots to the right (Rows 1 and 2). Hold the 1 cord out around a pin as shown and do the same on the opposite side of the seat. Alternate to the 3-4-5-6 position and tie one square knot to the left across Row 3. Pick up the looped-around cord 1 and tie Row 4 across in square knots to the right in the 1-2-3-4 position. Row 5 repeats Row 3, holding the 1 cord out around a pin again. Pick it up and tie a sennit of two square knots to the left in each set of four for Rows 6 and 7. Hold out 1 around the pin and tie a square knot to the right in the 3-4-5-6 configuration, straight across for Row 8. Pick up 1 and tie Row 9 straight across in square knots to the left in the 1-2-3-4 ends. Row 10 repeats Row 8. Rows 11 and 12 repeat Rows 1 and 2, etc. When the open area is filled, bring the short ends under the Frame up and over the core cords and to the underside again and tie them off. Take the long cords under the seat and to the underside of the lark's heads. Loop through and tie off on the underside. Bring the loops off the pins and with a length of extra twine, lace up, tie off. If you'll dip the ends of the cords in glue or at least tie an overhand knot in each one, the knotted area can be pulled taut again should it sag unmercifully.

16-4. To complete assembly, glue and nail on Back, rounding off edges, particularly the lower edge. Finish the whole chair same as Flat Seat Frame, then clamp and drill for the flathead wood screws used to attach the Seat to the Chair, locating the spacers neatly between Seat and Seat Frame.

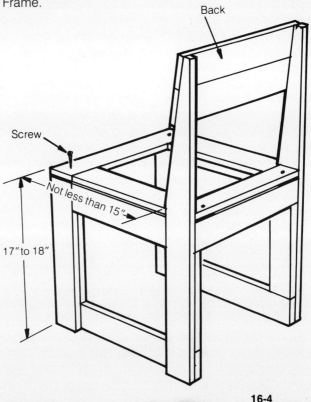

Back

Screw

Not less than 15"

17" to 18"

16-4

(Color Plate 3)

CHILD'S CHAIR

149

The child's chair is simply a scaled down version of the adult chair with a solid rather than a macrame seat. It is cut and put together in exactly the same way up to the seat part.

17-1. Cut and put together the Flat Seat Frame, sizing it as shown. The padded section we made of a scrap of ¼" plywood cut to lap over the opening and topped with a piece of 1" latex foam cut the same size with the corners undercut as indicated. The fabric on hand was a bit thin for this use so we reinforced it with an iron-on fusible interfacing, cut the same size as the plywood. Starting with the center of each side, the fabric was pulled taut over the foam and plywood and stapled fast. Working toward the corners, a

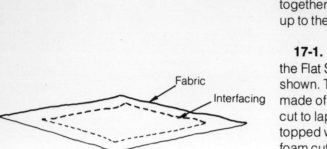

Fabric
Interfacing
Foam
Plywood

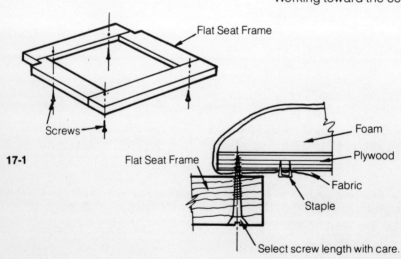

Flat Seat Frame

Screws

17-1

Flat Seat Frame

Foam

Plywood

Fabric

Staple

Select screw length with care.

17-1 Section

gently padded seat resulted. Holding it in position, flathead wood screws were run up through the Flat Seat Frame into the plywood to hold it on. Then the entire seat was nailed to the chair.

17-2.   Diagram is included to give dimensions for this size chair. If your child isn't this small, you can work out intermediate dimensions that may fit better, comparing these with the adult size chair shown in Project 16.

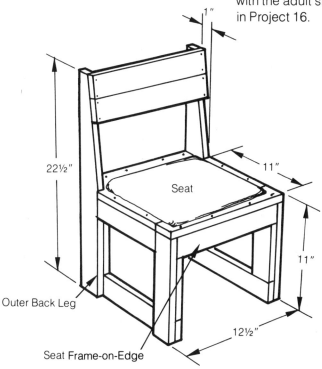

1"

22½"

11"

11"

Seat

Outer Back Leg

Seat Frame-on-Edge

12½"

17-2

(Color Plate 5)

ARMCHAIR

Though the Armchair and the Loveseat may look impressive, they are actually quite simple to build. With the use of your "C" clamps and a "try-it-first" approach, making the fabric covers may prove to be more work than the carpentry. Arithmetic still comes first but don't toss out your figures. The same ones will apply to the Loveseat too.

The proportions for this type of seating are given on the diagram on page 156. The thickness and size of the cushions you will use affect the size and location of frames and cleats which in turn have a bearing on the size Planked Frame Ends you will need, so start with the cushions.

You may buy ready-made ones (usually sold as replacements for loose-cushion furniture) or make you own. Twenty-one inches square by 4" or 5" thick for the seat cushion and 3" or 4" thick, 13" to 16" high and the same width as the seat are the usual dimensions. (Incidentally, the footstool will use the same size cushion as the back.) The cushions shown are 5" thick latex foam wrapped in two layers of quilt batting and covered in sturdy corduroy stitched into a simple envelope shape closed with hammer-on snap fasteners.

18-1. Both Seat and Back Frame Assemblies are made to a length ½" less overall than the width of the cushions for a snug fit. Seat Frame depth is the same as the seat cushion while the Back Frame Assembly is the cushion height plus the thickness of the Seat Cushion minus 2", if you round the cushion edges, 1" off if you use them square edged. Use a cleat width that will support the slats flush with the top of the frame-on-edge. Assemble the frame-on-edge, Cleats and Slats as shown, glue and nail together as you've done before (see Dog Bed page 79).

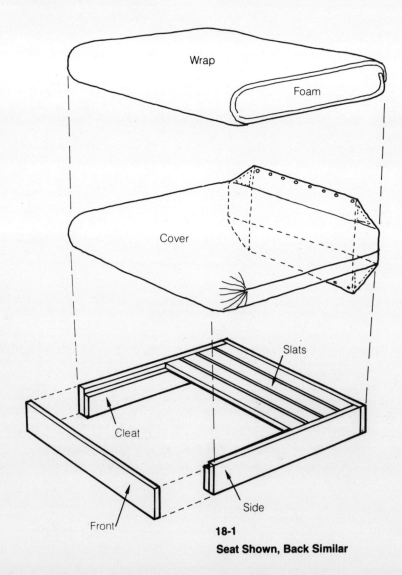

Wrap

Foam

Cover

Slats

Cleat

Side

Front

18-1

Seat Shown, Back Similar

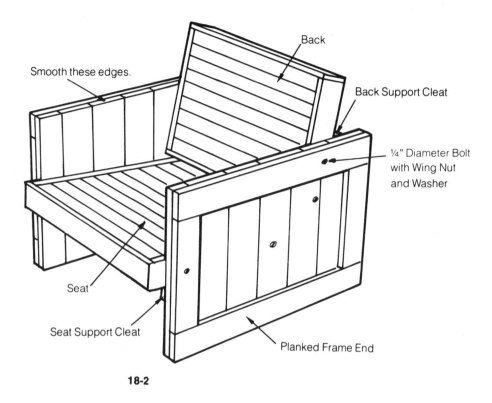

18-2

18-2. Determining the size of the Planked Frame Ends is next. You can do it on paper, using the dimensions shown in the diagram plus the information from your cushions and Seat and Back Frame Assemblies plus a knowledge of the width boards you have on hand. There is no exact size for the Ends except that they must be large enough to accommodate the Support Cleats you will use and the top edge or arm should be 5″ to 7″ above the upholstered seat height. This is a good time to really go all out on a "try-it-first" approach if you are unusually tall or unusually small. If you build your own chair, there is no reason you can't make it to fit you. You'll need some temporary supports to make a mock-up sturdy enough for you to sit in while you measure the results to establish the size of the Ends (see Chest page 113). Cut, glue and nail together the Planked Frame Ends. Smooth off carefully the top inner edge of these Ends where they act as chair arms.

Cut the Support Cleats over-length, and to double-check, clamp the Seat Support Cleat in position. Set the Seat Frame on it and mark the angle at which the ends of the Cleats should be cut for best appearance. Test out the Back Frame and its Support Cleats in the same manner and mark them for final cutting. Mark the inner surface of the Planked Frame Ends too, locating the Cleats. Remove the "C" clamps. Glue and nail the four Support Cleats in place, after you've cut them to final length. Clamp Seat and Back Frames in position. You will need eight ¼" machine-threaded bolts long enough to go through Ends and Seat and Back Frames with a washer and wing nut for each bolt. Place them and remove the "C" clamps. Now the chair is demountable for easier handling in finishing as well as in case you move.

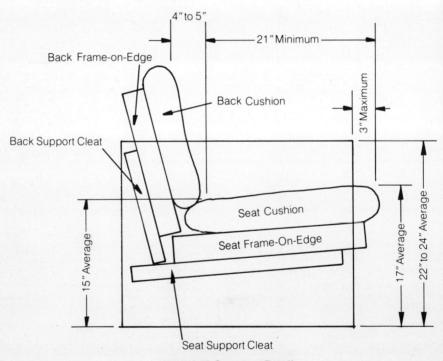

18 and 19 Common Detail

(Color Plate 5)

LOVESEAT

After that, building the Loveseat is a snap. Just think of it as a wider Armchair.

19-1. The two-cushion width suggests beefing up the Seat and Back Frames. Set an additional piece inside the Front and Back frame-on-edge members and add a Support Divider at the center of each frame. The overall lengths should equal the width of two cushions less 1″ for a snug fit.

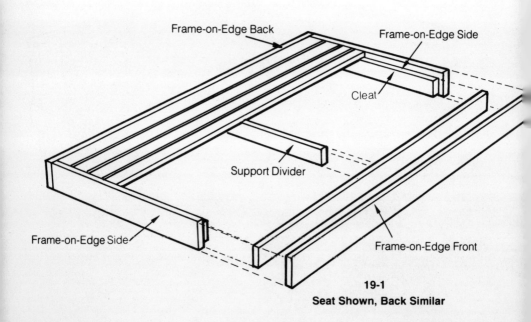

Frame-on-Edge Back

Frame-on-Edge Side

Cleat

Support Divider

Frame-on-Edge Side

Frame-on-Edge Front

19-1
Seat Shown, Back Similar

19-2. Size of the Planked Frame Ends and locations for the Support Cleats and the bolts will be the same as for the Armchair unless you are making the Loveseat to fit someone else.

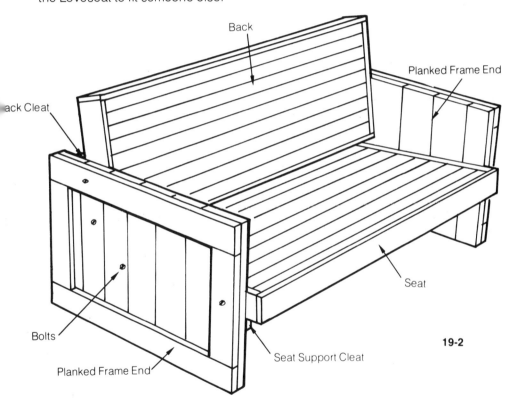

Back

Planked Frame End

Back Cleat

Seat

Bolts

Planked Frame End

Seat Support Cleat

19-2

Project 20

(Color Plate 5)

FOOTSTOOL

You've adapted the frame-on-edge with slats on top like the Dog Bed to a frame-on-edge with the slats inset flush like the Loveseat and Chair. You've been building Planked Frame Ends galore in Toy Chest, Modular Units and Armchair and Loveseat. With care in sawing, the two concepts can be further combined and the Cleat eliminated. So you can accomplish that easily, we suggest a simple jig.

20-1. To establish the size of the Planked Frame Ends, finish the footstool cushion first. We used the same size foam and batting wrap as the Back Cushions but left the cover open at both ends for a more symmetrical appearance. The top of the cushion should be about 1″ below the top of the cushioned chair seat, the top of the Planked Frame Ends will be the thickness of the cushion below that, which gives you the height of the Flat Frame Ends necessary. The width of the Flat Frame should be the same as the height of the back cushion. Glue and fasten the Flat Frames, one for each end of the stool.

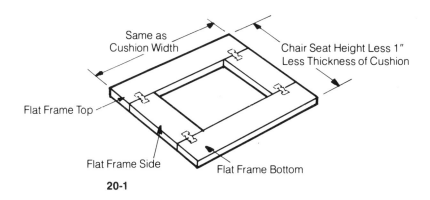

Same as Cushion Width

Chair Seat Height Less 1″ Less Thickness of Cushion

Flat Frame Top

Flat Frame Side

Flat Frame Bottom

20-1

20-2. Cut the Planks to equal the height of the Flat Frame less the thickness of the Slats. Figure how many are required to inset them the thickness of the External Battens, similar to the frame-on-edge used in the Chair and Child's Chair projects.

To make the jig, nail or clamp a scrap of 2x2 or something similar on top of your work space. Align the Flat Frame to it, top edge abutting the strip. Set a scrap strip, the same thickness as the Slat material, on edge on top of the Flat Frame and against the first Jig Strip. Tack that in place. Now set the cut Planks in place, butting them tightly against this second Jig Strip, at the same time maintaining the inset on both sides for the External Battens. Glue and nail the Planking to the Face Frame. Make two such Ends.

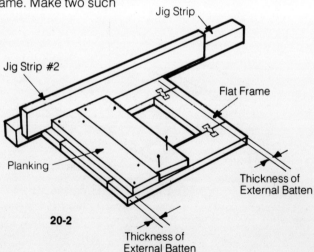

Jig Strip

Jig Strip #2

Flat Frame

Planking

Thickness of External Batten

Thickness of External Batten

20-2

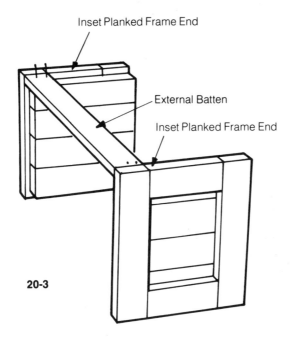

20-3

20-3. Cut Slats and External Battens to length of cushion less two times the thickness of the Flat Frame of the Ends. Lay the two Ends up on edge as shown and glue and nail the External Batten in place, flush with the top edge. Turn the stool over and glue and nail on the other Batten.

20-4. Set the stool upright and glue and nail the Slats in position, using the top edge of the planking in place of a Cleat. Put the cushion in place, put your feet on the cushion and relax.

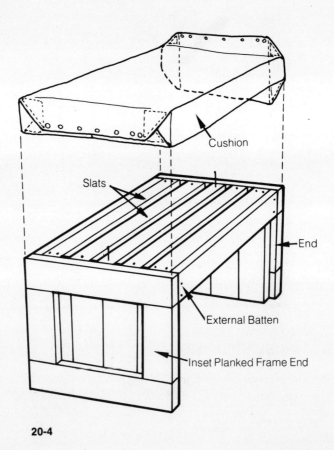

Cushion

Slats

End

External Batten

Inset Planked Frame End

20-4

(Color Plate 6)   # DESK

We've just seen how a part can sometimes be adjusted to serve more than one purpose. Design elements from two projects can also be re-combined to produce a third piece. The Desk is essentially a Drawered Unit (see page 126) combined with half a table (see page 89, 105 and 109).

The arithmetic of the drawer section is a bit different in approach. In the Module, we started from the shell size to arrive at the drawer parts dimensions. In the Desk, reverse that order: start with the file drawer and its hardware. Determine about what size you want (10" high by 12" wide clear inside drawer dimensions for 8½" x 11" letterhead files) and secure the hardware. Study and don't lose the installation instructions that come with it — they will most likely include clearance figures you need.

Some generally accepted average desk dimensions enter the picture too. Most desks are about 29" or 30" high. You need 24" or so for foot room. While an executive might rate a desk 36" from front to back (even larger for a First Vice President), a typical home desk will be built on a more modest scale, say 20" or 24" deep.

Sit down with pencil, paper, ruler and a knowledge of what wood you have available. Tackle the file drawer hardware first. You've bought it. Now build a drawer to fit it. For instance, we used an Amerock Tri-Roller Drawer Slide Set No. C-4047-2G which is for cabinets 18¼" inside dimension front to back and drawer lengths 16" or shorter. That's two dimensions established right there. (Exclude the False Front in figuring front to back dimensions.) The inside dimensions you want for the drawer, plus the thickness of the material you'll use to make it, plus the clearances noted on the installation instructions will tell you how wide to make your drawer case.

21-1.   The overall height of a desk less the thickness of a Planked Top (which you already know how to make, just make one to fit this Desk now) will give you the drawer case height. You know how to put the parts together. It's obvious from the drawing that only the top External Batten front and back need change to become one piece with the Apron of the Table design. Build the leg End the same way you built the Tea-for-Two Table and you have that solved. Run two long wood screws through the Planked Frame side of the drawer case into the end of the Cross Brace and you've anchored that. A desk will usually have a smaller overhang than a table top, so try for a minimal dimension there. You've located battens for a top before. Use at least three for a desk top. Put it together, installing drawer pulls and hardware following the manufacturer's instructions, set the top on and get to work. One of your dining chairs can do double duty while you sit at the desk figuring out the arithmetic for the bed project.

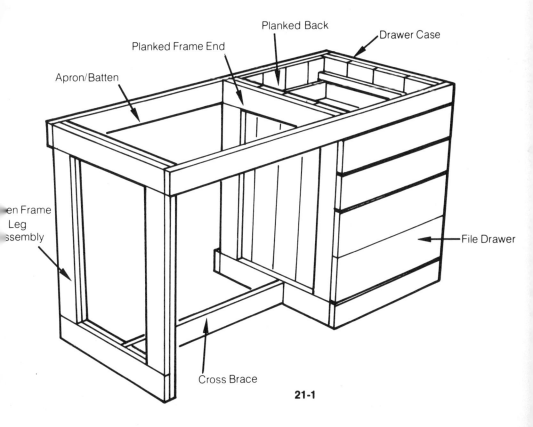

Planked Back

Drawer Case

Planked Frame End

Apron/Batten

en Frame
Leg
ssembly

File Drawer

Cross Brace

21-1

Project 22

BED

168

A bedstead is one of those pieces of furniture you can do without but when the day finally comes that you want to get the mattress up off the floor, there are a number of ways. A simple 2x6 frame-on-edge affixed to the underside of your box-springs and mattress is perhaps the simplest; or you could buy a metal Hollywood frame. The next step up would be to build yourself a headboard.

22-1. You could build a simple frame-on-edge of 4″ to 6″ wide crate lumber with at least one vertical divider inside. Placed against the wall, the larger area is closed over with a Planked Frame. How big depends on the width of your bed and the size of material used for the Flat Frame. It looks best if the inner edge of the Flat Frame fits fairly close to the width of the made-up bed. The

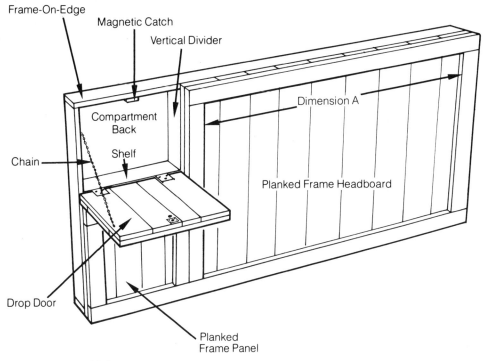

Frame-On-Edge
Magnetic Catch
Vertical Divider
Compartment Back
Chain
Shelf
Dimension A
Planked Frame Headboard
Drop Door
Planked Frame Panel

22-1

smaller area will accommodate a drop-door night table with another Planked Frame Panel closing in the space below it. Overall height and height of door in down position, etc. are all interdependent, affected by the top of a made-up bed and whether you want to use a wedge bolster at the head. We used a 33″ overall height with a 14″ high door which when opened provides a level surface 19″ above the floor.

22-1. Detail. For the drop-leaf night table you will need a pair of hinges for a flush overlay door and a magnetic catch as well as a pull and some lightweight chain. Use a piece of plywood or hardboard to close the back of the night-table compartment, gluing and nailing it in place from the back. Plan on adding a facing piece below the horizontal Shelf member, as you will have to allow the thickness of the Planked-Frame Door to clear the panel below. Figure this after you get the hinge. Hinge and catch as well as pull will follow the manufacturer's instructions for installation. (Check the length of the screws supplied. You have an extra-thick door to work on.) The chain may be held with screweyes or hooks to control the leveling of the drop-down door.

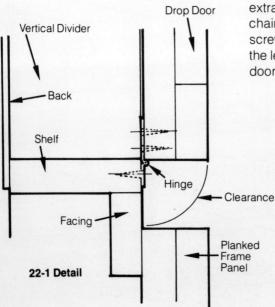

Vertical Divider

Drop Door

Back

Shelf

Hinge

Clearance

Facing

Planked Frame Panel

22-1 Detail

22-2. To build the whole unit as shown, from scratch, you will need a 5″ thick twin-size foam mattress and a piece of ½″ thick plywood 2″ wider and 1″ longer than the mattress. Chances of finding a piece that large are not very good but you might be lucky or you may consider it worthwhile to check prices on bed boards sold for bunk beds. If you already have an innerspring mattress that can be supported on slats, that too will work, though check out the total height dimensions carefully. It is usually desirable to enclose only the bottom inch or so of the mattress for ease in making up a bed. The top of the made-up bed is usually kept about 17″ or 18″ above the floor. The exact height will depend on the width boards you can find in the longer lengths required.

When you have combined all this information, the total width of the finished bed Enclosure Frame will determine Dimension A of the Headboard. (We warned you, half the work of using crate lumber is figuring out how best to use what you've scrounged. Beds are simple to build, they just take some arithmetic.)

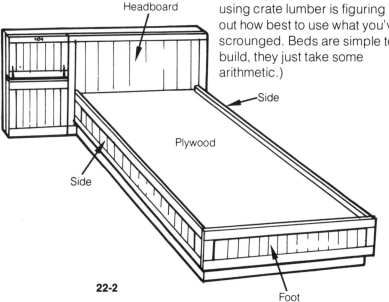

22-2

Headboard · Side · Plywood · Side · Foot

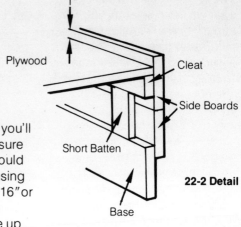

22-2. Detail. From the boards you have on hand, you'll have to work out the Enclosure construction in detail. It should run somewhat as shown, using Short Battens about every 16" or 18" to hold the two or three boards you'll need to make up the proper height.

1"
Plywood
Cleat
Side Boards
Short Batten
22-2 Detail
Base

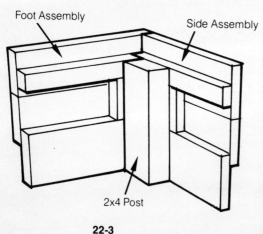

Foot Assembly
Side Assembly
2x4 Post
22-3

22-3. Viewed from inside the Enclosure without the plywood in place, how Foot Assembly and Side Assemblies meet all depends. Once you've determined the size Enclosure Frame you need, the next decision is another one only you can make. Is this to be a built-in, forever enshrined in one location? Then glue and nail all the joints. Is it to be moved when you move, perhaps two or three times in its lifetime? You can make it up as a frame, gluing and nailing the 2x4 posts shown into position and bolting the Headboard Plate to the Headboard (see 22-4) or you can make four separate sections with the 2x4 posts attached to a Headboard Plate Assembly (glued and nailed to the headboard) and one on each Side Assembly as shown here. Then use flathead wood screws through the Sides into the Headboard Posts and through the Foot Assembly into the Side Posts.

22-4. If you're on the move every few months, look into the loose-pin hinge method, here seen from inside the enclosure without the plywood in place. Glue and nail up Foot and Sides as separate units and glue and nail the Headboard Plate to the Headboard. Do not use the 2x4 posts. Assemble the four parts,

clamping them in squared up, level position. Attach a regular loose-pin door hinge in position as shown at each corner. Then knock the pins out and you're back to four parts — Headboard, two Sides and a Foot — easily realigned, provided you do not lose the hinge pins in the move.

Note: If your room plan requires a night table to the left of the bed, just put it there. Construction remains the same. If you followed the arithmetic for sizing the bed enclosure section, you will know how to go at it if you want a place to sleep two. The double-bed width, if

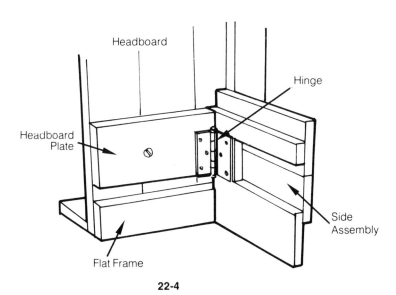

Headboard

Hinge

Headboard Plate

Side Assembly

Flat Frame

22-4

you plan to use a foam mattress on plywood, will require additional support at the plywood edges, and the wider headboard should have an added support within the center section.

Otherwise, proceed as described for a twin bed. For one or for two, when you have it all assembled again, get out your new bedding and make up the bed. Crawl in and take a well-deserved rest.

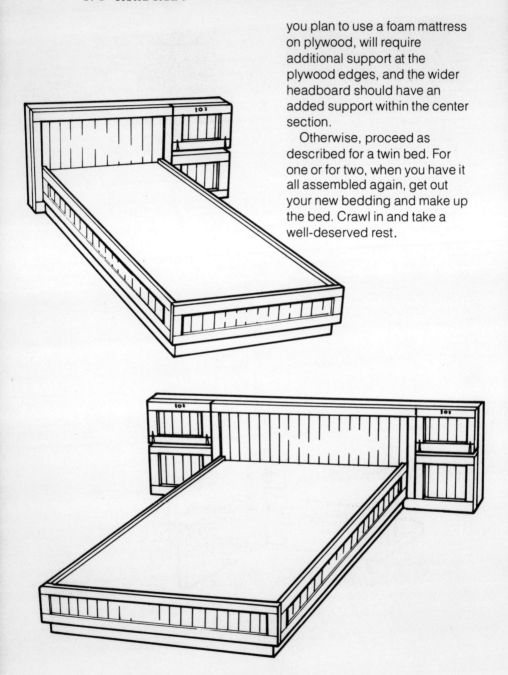

MAKING IT ALL WORTHWHILE

FINISHING IT ALL UP

Paint does not make wood smooth and no amount of stain will make pine look like anything but pine with some stain on it. These two facts of life may well summarize this section.

You are going to sit in, lie and work on, eat and relax at the furniture you've built. Sooner or later parts of it will come in contact with you or your clothes. The boards were undoubtedly not too smooth when you found them, may have been splintered up a bit more in salvage and probably are not completely without uncomfortable edges yet, though we hope you've smoothed off the worst places as you stacked the raw material before you built anything at all with it.

The first thing to do when you've finished any one project is to check it out all over for major cracks, splits or splinters that may have developed during construction. Round off the too-sharp edge, smooth down the shaggy saw-cut end. Your power sander with the coarse grit sandpaper first, followed by medium and then by fine will

175

make the surfaces about as smooth as they are going to get. How smooth that is will depend on the kind and the cut of wood you've used and the length of time you devote to smoothing it.

To cover well with anything, most noticeably if you want to change the color, you must have the surface not only smooth but clean. No glue stains, no oil, no grease and no sanding dust. A good wipe-down with lacquer thinner is one way. At least a good brush-off for the minimum treatment.

It is well to caution, before you get too far, that paints and finishes and their solvents (other than water base) are all highly flammable and should not be treated sloppily if you want to avoid going off with a bang. Good ventilation doesn't hurt either in avoiding just going off. You've already found out how helpful used newspaper is as a sound-deadening padding. It is also pretty good for absorbing liquids. With plastic film down first, covered with a "blotter" of newsprint, you could even finish furniture safely in the living room of a hotel suite. (Inadvisable — newspaper does not blot up the smell.) Plastic film is great for catching splatters but scuffs up and punctures too easily to be walked around on much, hence the newspaper suggestion. Also, did you ever try to fold a 10'x12' plastic drop with a pint's worth of puddle on it? And save cans for mixing colors, but don't can your dirty paint rags.

You are making practical, rough but useable, simple but attractive furniture. You are not doing fine cabinet making and this is not the place for a padded, hand-rubbed French polish. It is the right place for the quick and easy, colorful yet durable, economical and available finish. Exactly which one is the question.

If the wood in its natural, weathered state, is attractive and not too uncomfortable to handle, leave it alone, in accessories at least. If you've got it reasonably smooth and like the looks of it, use a penetrating resin wood finish that you can brush on; let it set and sink in and then wipe off any left unabsorbed. Follow the directions on the can. It will change the color of the wood about as much as water does. The light reflectance is changed, and on a rough-sawed face this can make quite a difference in appearance. The number of coats you'll need will depend on the wood's surface and on the position of its use — a table top should have more protection than the back of a cabinet would really require.

If you like the protection of resin but not the color of the wood you have, and you want to tint the wood without losing the grain, then a dye-type stain is what to look for. And you will have to look, probably to mail-order sources. Water-soluble analine dyes will raise the grain and non-grain-raising dye type stains aren't usually used on the very kinds of wood you're most apt to have found. These would almost always require at least three coats of resin sealer or varnish to protect them.

Much easier to handle and to find for sale — and actually much more suitable for this style of furniture — are the pigmented wiping stains. These concoctions have the colored pigment suspended (not dissolved) in the vehicle, and that pigment lodges in any roughness of the surface. Scratches and dents, the softwood grain, cracks and places where you didn't sand too well pick up the colorant. You do have to stir these stains constantly to keep the pigment suspended evenly, but they are about as easy to use as possible. Use a trick my father used and the application is even simpler. Fold over a clean carpet scrap and hold it with a

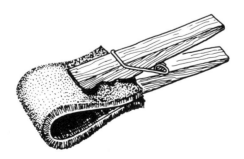

spring-type clothespin and you have an ideal tailor-made, disposable applicator. Your safest move is to follow the directions on the can. How soon you wipe and how hard you rub control the deepness of the color developed. Again, protective coats of varnish or more resin over the stain are still a good idea though in some places on some surfaces a coat of wax may be enough. Two coats of varnish over the pigmented wiping stains will usually replace the three coats needed with the dye-type stains though. Both the "walnut" and the grey "barnwood" colors we used were pigmented wiping stains but don't believe color labels without knowing the manufacturers' names. "Walnut" from three sources is still going to be three different shades of brown on the same piece of pine. Test out the color you choose on scrap first. It is even safer to give that scrap at least one coat of the protective varnish or resin coating you intend to use, as the looks will again vary a bit.

If you've really got the wood smooth and want a once-over-lightly deal you can use a varnish stain combining a stain colorant and a varnish vehicle, but it is really a cheap way out, and it will look it. With this type of coating on the uneven color you are bound to get with scrap wood, you lose the chance to make the extra-light board a bit darker that wiping a bit more stain on that board gives you. If you are in a hurry, a varnish stain on inside surfaces might work out, but for places that show, it is far safer to go to a two-stage job — stain for color, then varnish to protect. Actually, if you want that color, you can stain your wood with very much thinned-out enamel paint, then varnish the piece.

But *really* painting the kind of wood you are apt to have found to work with is going to require a lot more sanding. You need a really smooth texture on a really level surface to begin with. Use a satin rather than a high-gloss enamel, but only after you give the raw wood a sealer coat. If the surface feels prickly rough after that, sand some more and give it another coat. Otherwise, each little fiber standing up on end is going to get painted in that position. When you are satisfied, prime with the proper undercoater for the kind of paint you're using. If you have a strong color for the finish coat, it's a good idea to tint your undercoater with a bit of it.

BLENDING IT ALL IN

But what color? We're not about to dictate decoration schemes to you. Your own taste will lead you to any number of possible combinations. With the wood fairly decent and left "woody" looking, the pieces can be combined with bright, true colors in upholstery, rug and wall colors for quite a modern look. The lines of the pieces are simple and honest enough to warrant consideration in a natural contemporary setting. They're plain enough to fit well into any primitive or country-style decor, too. Round the edges a bit more for that "worn" look and experiment with shading to make instant antiques. With the colonial hardware in wrought iron finish, you'll have an Early American-style piece. If you've done a reasonably good job and have the surfaces fairly well smoothed, wiping on a mahogany tone and using any of the simpler styles of hardware, the pieces will fit into more traditional schemes. With larger-scale brass hardware and a deeper-tone stain, the same pieces will work in a Mediterranean decor. We played it middle-of-the-road with a style in antique brass. You will want to give a great deal of thought to the details that go to make a decorative scheme yours. We've suggested in the lighting projects how your choice of basic materials might make these decorative accessories fit into your scheme while using the construction methods shown. You'll have to make this kind of decision about everything.

PLANNING IT IN THE FIRST PLACE

To build furniture that will do what you want it to, first find out what you want done. Then see how much room you've got to do it in. Making a floor plan or furniture plot may seem like a lot of work, but it is a lot easier to move little pieces of cardboard around on a piece of graph paper than it is to hoist heavy furniture back and forth while you "see if it fits."

To take a typical (hypothetical) situation, let's say you've just found an empty two-room apartment and it is three weeks until you have to move in. You have your quad system, record collection, two loose drawing boards and a footlocker full of.bedding to furnish it with. The apartment's kitchen consists of ten feet along one wall, with refrigerator, sink and range in a row, wall-hung cabinets over the appliances. As you'll come to know only too well, that leaves two minuscule patches of countertop but at least the clothes closets are ample.

First, get a large sheet of graph paper, either eight or four squares to the inch. Let each ¼" square on the paper be equal to 1'0" square of space in the apartment. (It is easier if you use the 8 squares per inch. Then each little square equals 6 inches.) Draw on the paper the outline of the space you want to consider, indicating doors, windows, permanently built-in features (including the riser to the radiator upstairs) and electrical outlets and fixtures. Show which way the doors swing (include the refrigerator door). There are times when it will be nice to know how much room the oven door takes up when it is left open, and if the base cabinets have hinged doors, note their swing too. In the diagram are some symbols shown in an imaginary plan so you can see what some of the indications in architectural sketch plans mean.

Assigning a thickness to the walls can sometimes make a difference. You *know* they are more than a line thick. You may not know exactly how thick they are. Interior walls of plasterboard on studs really measure about 5" (3⅝" for the stud, ¾" and ¾" for the plaster, which adds up to 5¼"). You won't be far wrong if you indicate interior partitions as 6" thick. In a tight corner, when inches matter, you may have

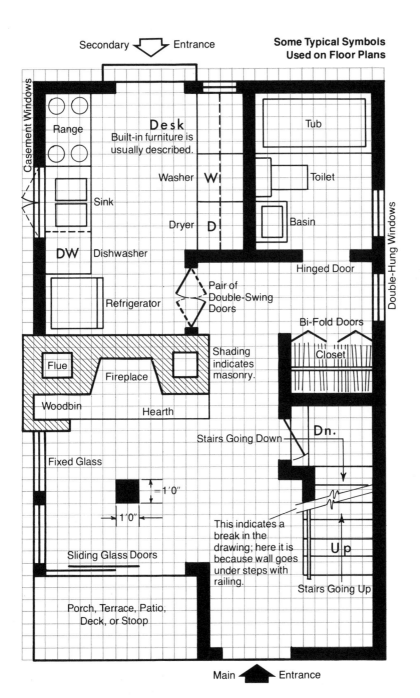

Secondary ⬰ Entrance

**Some Typical Symbols
Used on Floor Plans**

Casement Windows

Range

Desk
Built-in furniture is
usually described.

Washer W

Dryer D

Sink

DW Dishwasher

Refrigerator

Pair of
Double-Swing
Doors

Tub

Toilet

Basin

Hinged Door

Double-Hung Windows

Bi-Fold Doors

Closet

Shading
indicates
masonry.

Flue

Fireplace

Woodbin

Hearth

Stairs Going Down

Dn.

Fixed Glass

=1′0″

1′0″

This indicates a
break in the
drawing; here it is
because wall goes
under steps with
railing.

Up

Sliding Glass Doors

Stairs Going Up

Porch, Terrace, Patio,
Deck, or Stoop

Main ⬆ Entrance

to make more accurate measurements of the trim around doors, etc., but for sketching the indications given are good enough. Measure and mark until you have an accurate representation of your apartment floor plan made to scale on the large sheet. Go over your pencil lines in ink.

Now the fun part. Use cardboard (in different colors if you want to) to indicate movable furnishings. You'll need the outline of the floor plan showing the space each piece of furniture occupies. Keeping the pieces of furniture represented by moving pieces of cardboard will enable you to see if there is room to push the chair back from the table, room to get the footstool in front of the other chair. You can, if you want to, go so far as to paste another piece of paper to those cardboards representing pieces with doors that open or drawers that pull out to show the limits of those spatial requirements.

Now think. If you already have some furniture, make cutouts for those pieces too. Take a look at the projects shown here and decide what you'd like to work with, what pieces best suit your needs. At the end of the chapter we've shown outlines for each piece included in this book. They're drawn at the ¼" to 1'0" scale and show the average dimension to aim for, though you may decide on narrower or wider where a project is based on actual dimensions, depending on widths of boards used.

MAKING THE PIECES FIT THE PUZZLE

Once you have the cutouts made, you need to think about the spaces between. How much room do you need between coffee table and settee? (Twelve inches.) Between open drawer and foot of the bed? (Eighteen inches.) Between an open drawer and a wall you'll need more like 30". (Stand up and bend over, pretending to pull out a bottom drawer. You'll see why there's a difference.) To get between an occupied chair at the table and the wall behind it, you need 30". To sit down takes about the same.

Playing around with the cutout pieces will show you right away that if the head of the bed is there, against that wall, you'll have to walk all the way around it to get from the closet to the bath.

Whatever you decide, whatever you ultimately build, will be yours, tailored to your needs and finished to fit your scheme. Sit down, enjoy and decide what you'll build next.

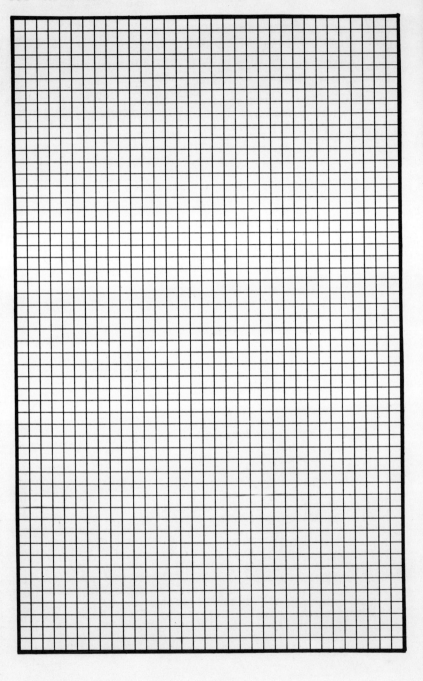

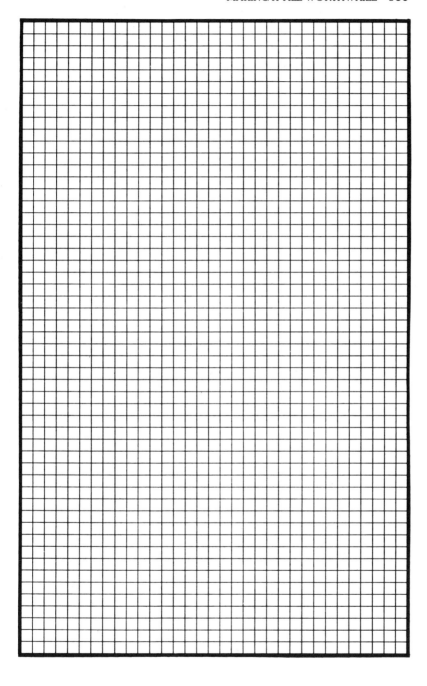

Outlines for Planning Cutouts

All sizes shown as built. Yours may be a bit different.

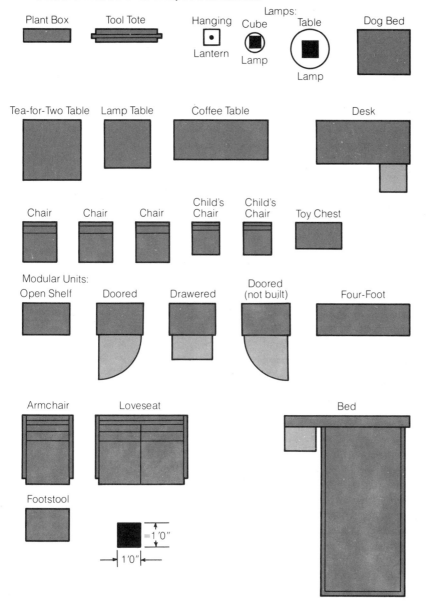

INFORMATIVE EXTRAS

SOURCES OF SUPPLIES AND INFORMATION

While your local hardware, lumber and /or home center store will have nails, screws, cabinetware and the other bits and pieces necessary for completing the projects shown, you may want more definite source information for the exact items shown or mentioned in this book. Other brands are available. Those listed are intended only as suggestions for those wishing to follow exactly the plans given. Note that manufacturers do not usually sell by mail to retail customers. They can, however, usually direct you to a source that can supply you. We list below the product and the manufacturer, where a specific item was included in this book.

Cabinetware and
drawer slide

Amerock Corp.
4000 Auburn St.
Rockford, Ill. 61101

Lamparts®
lighting accessories

Angelo Brothers Co.
159 West Allegheny Ave.
Philadelphia, Penna. 19154

Surform® and other hand and power tools	Stanley Tools Division of The Stanley Works New Britain, Conn. 06050
Plexiglas® acrylic plastic	Rohm and Haas Independence Mall West Philadelphia, Penna. 19105
Skotch® fasteners	Superior Fastener Corp. 9536 West Foster Ave. Chicago, Ill. 60656
Teenut® fasteners	United-Carr Supply Division TRW Inc. 1 Nevada St. Newtonville, Mass. 02160
Glue	Franklin Glue Co. 2020 Bruck Columbus, O. 43207

Tools, cabinetware and many specialty items are readily available by mail order from the following companies. Write to them directly, requesting the cost of their current catalogs.

Albert Constantine
2056 Eastchester Rd.
Bronx, N.Y. 10461

Craftsman Wood Service
2729 South Mary St.
Chicago, Ill. 60608

Minnesota Woodworkers Supply Co.
Industrial Blvd.
Rogers, Minn. 55374

Both Sears, Roebuck's and Montgomery Ward's catalogs include many of these items, too.

The fusible interfacing we used on the dog bed pillow

and the child's chair seat is Suit-Weight Easy Shaper® by:

> Stacy Fabrics Corp.
> 469 Seventh Ave.
> New York, N.Y. 10018

The Mini-crates used decoratively in the color photos come from:

> TACC Industries
> 66 Newark Pompton Turnpike
> Riverdale, N.J. 07457

Information can also be obtained from sources and suppliers not previously mentioned.

Many trade associations are the source of helpful information on how to select and how to work with the products processed or manufactured by their member companies. Most will usually send a price list of available consumer literature. It's a good idea to send a stamped, self-addressed envelope with your request.

American Plywood Association
1119 A St.
Tacoma, Wash. 98401

California Redwood Association
617 Montgomery St.
San Francisco, Cal. 94111

National Forest Products Association
1619 Massachusetts Ave. NW
Washington, D.C. 20036

National Paint and Coatings Association
1500 Rhode Island Ave. NW
Washington, D.C. 20005

Western Wood Products Association
1500 Yeon Building
Portland, Ore. 97204

Some of the larger manufacturers will send you a list of the consumer literature they offer; again a stamped, self-addressed envelope is a good idea. In addition to excellent, instructive booklets from Angelo Brothers, Rohm and Haas and Stanley (see previous listing of manufacturers whose products were used in the projects shown) we have seen fine material from the following companies.

Clamps and clamping: Adjustable Clamp Co.
411 North Ashland Ave.
Chicago, Ill. 60622

Use and care of certain
mechanic's hand tools: Crescent Tool Co.
The Cooper Group
P.O. Box 728
Apex, N.C. 27502

Care and use of saws and
files: Nicholson File Co.
P.O. Box 6488
Providence, R.I. 02904

Working with Masonite®
hardboard: Masonite Corp.
29 North Wacker Dr.
Chicago, Ill. 60606

Wood finishing: Benjamin Moore and Co.
Chestnut Ridge Rd.
Montvale, N.J. 07645

The Flecto Co. Inc.
1000 45th
Oakland, Cal. 94607

McCloskey Varnish Co.
7600 State Rd.
Philadelphia, Penna. 19136

The Minwax Company
72 Oak
Clifton, N.J. 07014

In addition to The Stanley Company, some other companies that make power tools are:

Black and Decker Mfg. Co.
Towson, Md. 21204

Rockwell International
Power Tool Division
3171 Directors Row
Memphis, Tenn. 38131

Skil Corp.
5033 Elston Ave.
Chicago, Ill. 60630

METRIC EQUIVALENCY CHART

CONVERTING INCHES TO CENTIMETERS

mm=millimeters   cm=centimeters   m=meters

CHANGING INCHES TO MILLIMETERS AND CENTIMETERS
(Slightly rounded for your convenience.)

inches	mm	cm	inches	cm	inches	cm
⅛	3mm		7	18	29	73.5
¼	6mm		8	20.5	30	76
⅜	10mm or	1cm	9	23	31	79
½	13mm or	1.3cm	10	25.5	32	81.5
⅝	15mm or	1.5cm	11	28	33	84
¾	20mm or	2cm	12	30.5	34	86.5
⅞	22mm or	2.2cm	13	33	35	89
1	25mm or	2.5cm	14	35.5	36	91.5
1¼	32mm or	3.2cm	15	38	37	94
1½	38mm or	3.8cm	16	40.5	38	96.5
1¾	45mm or	4.5cm	17	43	39	99
2	50mm or	5cm	18	46	40	101.5
2½	65mm or	6.5cm	19	48.5	41	104
3	75mm or	7.5cm	20	51	42	106.5
3½	90mm or	9cm	21	53.5	43	109
4	100mm or	10cm	22	56	44	112
4½	115mm or	11.5cm	23	58.5	45	114.5
5	125mm or	12.5cm	24	61	46	117
5½	140mm or	14cm	25	63.5	47	119.5
6	150mm or	15cm	26	66	48	122
			27	68.5	49	124.5
			28	71	50	127

HOW BIG IS A NAIL?

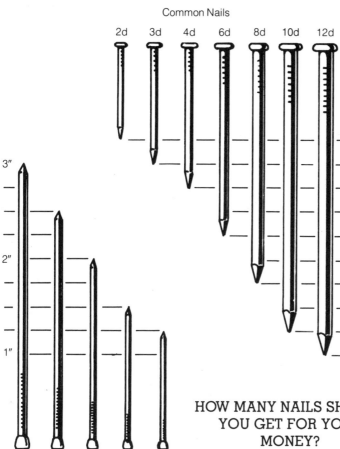

Common Nails

2d 3d 4d 6d 8d 10d 12d 16d

3″ 2″ 1″ 1″ 2″ 3″

10d 8d 6d 4d 3d

Finishing Nails

HOW MANY NAILS SHOULD YOU GET FOR YOUR MONEY?

		Number per Pound	
Penny Number	Length in Inches	Common Nails	Finishing Nails
2	1	876	1351
3	1¼	568	807
4	1½	316	548
5	1¾	271	500
6	2	181	309
8	2½	106	189
10	3	69	121
12	3¼	64	113
16	3½	49	90
20	4	31	62
30	4½	20	

FROM THE WIRE
TO THE WALL

One thing often overlooked in building for the home is how to get what you build to hang on a wall hung on a wall. First, you must determine what kind of wall you are faced with. It may be solid masonry, in which case concrete nails can be used to attach a wood strip that will provide an anchorage for a simple shelf.

If it's the mirror (page 85) you wish to hang, you'll need a metal hook with one or two screw holes. To hold the screws that go through these holes, some type of expansion-plug anchor must first be inserted in the masonry wall. You will probably need a star drill to make the oversized hole required. The package the anchors come in usually contains instructions and will tell you how large to make the hole.

To install a fiber screw anchor, drill the hole first and clean it out. Insert the plug and push it all the way in. Hold the hook in position and put the screw through the hole in the hook into the plug. As you tighten the screw the plug will expand against the sides of the hole, securing the hook.

If your walls are not solid, but hollow, of plaster on lath, plasterboard, thin panels of plywood, or even hollow

196

concrete blocks or tile, all hope is not lost. The older method involved a toggle bolt. For this,one drilled a hole through the thin-wall large enough to shove a folded toggle bolt through to a point where gravity pulled the wing-bar into position, or where its design caused it to spring into position. Tightening the bolt brought the anchor end up tight against the backside of the thin-wall. If you wanted to install a hook with this type of device you set the hook on the bolt, then replaced the wings before you shoved the toggle bolt into the hole in the wall.

An improvement on the toggle bolt is the patented multiple wing device. You insert such a device into an oversize hole, tighten the screw, and then the umbrella-like ribs fold up against the back of the thin-wall, holding the anchor in place. You can then remove the screws, position the hook or whatever it is you want to attach, and reinsert the screw in the same anchor.

Of course you can avoid all this hardware use if you live in a frame structure, and can find a framing member in the right place for the hanging device you wish to attach. There are magnetic stud finders on the market guaranteed to steer you to a stud if you can magnetize a nail; there are vibrator-type stud finders guaranteed to find you the stud if you continually hit the wall hard enough to make the little ball bounce. All you really need is a bony knuckle and an accurate ear. Listen for a change in tone as you tap your way horizontally across the wall. When every sixteen inches you hear the same different tone, that's where the stud is. Once in a while in an older house you'll find twenty-four inch spacing. But sixteen inches is presently more common and the same spacing holds for ceiling joists. Now all you have to do is make sure that the screw is long enough so that the threaded portion is secured in the wood member. Remember this when you're hanging the lantern.